# THE BLUEPRINT HACK

Smart DIY Series

Published by ADAPT Publishing



Published by ADAPT Publishing

ISBN: 978-1-971231-06-8

Editor: Angie Diaz
Cover design and layout: Vicki Ramírez Fraga

SMART DIY: BOOK I

# THE BLUEPRINT HACK

*Outsource the Red Tape, DIY the Build, and Save Thousands on Your ADU.*

# Content

# INTRODUCTION

## The Design-Driven Advantage

Building an Accessory Dwelling Unit (ADU) in Southern California is an exciting prospect for many homeowners. An ADU can create extra living space, generate rental income, or offer a comfortable home for family members. However, for most people, that excitement fades once they learn how expensive the process can be. A fully finished ADU built by a contractor can easily cost over $300,000, making the project feel out of reach or financially unfeasible.

This book introduces a different and much more accessible option: the Design-Driven DIY ADU. Despite the name, this method does not require you to be a construction expert or perform all the work yourself. Instead, it focuses on strategic budgeting. The core idea is to invest money upfront by hiring professionals for design, engineering, and permitting so that the construction phase becomes simpler, clearer, and much less risky for the homeowner.

In this approach, your team of professionals—the architect, the engineer, and the permit expediter—works together to guide the project much like a general contractor would, but before any building begins. They prepare complete, code-approved, and carefully reviewed plans that act as a detailed roadmap. These plans reduce confusion, prevent costly mistakes, and make every construction step easier to manage.

By investing in this strong planning foundation, you can avoid hiring a traditional General Contractor (GC), who typically charges high fees to oversee the project. Skipping the GC doesn't mean cutting corners; it means you are stepping into the role of manager with clear, professional guidance in hand. This can save you tens of thousands of dollars while still guaranteeing the safety, quality, and legal compliance

of your ADU.

The biggest difference between this method and a typical "hybrid" build—where a GC handles only the basic structure—is who manages the project. With the Design-Driven DIY approach, you, the homeowner, oversee the entire build from start to finish site preparation, framing, utilities, and final finishes. But you are not doing it alone. You are following a thorough, professional blueprint that removes the guesswork and gives you the confidence to make informed decisions.

This trade-off—paying more upfront for design in exchange for major savings during construction—is what makes this model so effective. It is perfect for homeowners who want more control over their budget, wish to avoid unnecessary markups, and prefer to keep the project on their own timeline.

This guide will walk you through the entire journey, step by step—from shaping your vision to navigating permits and completing construction—until the day you receive your final Certificate of Occupancy and officially finish your ADU.

# PART I

## BEFORE YOU START ANYTHING

CHAPTER 1

# Defining Your ADU Vision

Before you hire anyone or start sketching ideas, the most important step is to clearly define the purpose of your ADU. This early clarity becomes the foundation of the entire Design-Driven DIY approach. When you know exactly why you are building the ADU and how you plan to use it, every subsequent decision becomes easier, smarter, and more cost-effective.

Understanding the ADU's function—whether it will house a family member, serve as a rental unit, become a guest suite, or act as a future downsizing option—helps your design and engineering team focus their efforts. These professionals are an investment and giving them clear direction ensures they do not waste time (or your money) designing something that does not truly fit your needs.

A well-defined vision also helps you avoid costly redesigns and prevents surprises later in the process. When your purpose is clear from the beginning, you end up with an ADU that not only meets today's needs but also supports your long-term goals, making the entire investment more valuable and satisfying.

## Functionality First: Purpose Dictates Design

The most important factor in shaping your ADU is its function. How you plan to use the space will determine its size, layout, and the features included inside. When the purpose is clear, the design naturally follows. Here are a few common uses and what they typically require:

- **Rental Income:** If your goal is to rent out the ADU, the design should focus on durability and low maintenance. Renters do not need luxury finishes; they need practical, reliable ones. A simple floor plan, standard fixtures, and materials that are easy to clean or replace will keep costs down and appeal to a wide range of tenants. The goal here is efficiency, longevity, and broad market appeal.
- **Family Use (In-Law Unit, Adult Child, Guest House):** If the ADU is meant for a family member, you have the freedom to tailor the design to their specific needs. This could include features like step-free entrances, wider doorways, grab bars, extra storage, or even a layout that allows for some connection to the main house. The emphasis here is on comfort, accessibility, and long-term livability.
- **Home Office or Creative Studio**: If the ADU will function as a workspace, the design should support productivity. Natural light, good ventilation, and effective soundproofing become priorities. High-speed internet access is essential, and you may not need a full kitchen—eliminating it can save both space and money. In this case, the ADU becomes more like a professional environment than a traditional living unit.

Understanding your ADU's primary purpose early on helps

you avoid unnecessary features, manage your budget wisely, and create a space that truly serves its intended use.

## Size and Layout Optimization

Although California state law guarantees that you can build an ADU of at least 800 square feet, bigger is not always better. Many homeowners assume that maximizing square footage automatically increases value, but a smaller, well-planned ADU can dramatically cut costs while still feeling spacious and livable. Choosing the right size— and designing an efficiency layout—can save thousands of dollars without sacrificing comfort.

## The 500-750 Sq. Ft.

**"Sweet Spot":** For many ADU projects, this size range offers the best blend of affordability and functionality. A unit between 500 and 750 square feet can comfortably fit a one-bedroom layout or even a compact two- bedroom design. It provides enough room for everyday living without driving up costs for materials, labor, and utilities. This size is also easier to heat, cool, and maintain, which keeps long-term expenses down.

**Layout Efficiency:** Square footage is only part of the equation; how that space is organized matters just as much. Work closely with your designer to eliminate unnecessary hallways or awkward corners that do not serve a purpose. Open-concept living areas can make a smaller ADU feel larger and more welcoming.

Consider using vertical space for storage, such as tall cabinets or built-in shelving, to keep the floor area open and flexible. An efficient layout ensures that every square foot works hard and supports the ADU's intended use.

By focusing on smart sizing and thoughtful design, you can create an ADU that feels spacious, functions beautifully, and stays within budget.

## Aesthetics: Matching vs. Modern

Choosing the exterior look of your ADU is not just about personal style; it can also affect your budget, your permitting timeline, and the overall complexity of the project. While both traditional and modern designs can work beautifully, it is important to understand how each choice may influence costs and construction. Matching the Main House: Some homeowners want their ADU to look like a natural extension of the main home. This can mean matching the roof shape, exterior siding, trim details, and window style. The result is visually cohesive and can help the ADU blend seamlessly into the property. However, this approach can sometimes add complexity. Older homes often have design elements that are more difficult or expensive to replicate, such as unusual roof angles or custom materials. While the final look may be worth it, it typically requires more detailed planning and may increase both design and construction costs. Modern Design: A more modern ADU—often a clean, rectangular shape with simple lines—tends to be the most budget-friendly option. These designs usually feature flat or gently sloped shed-style roofs, straightforward framing, and minimal exterior detailing. Because the structure is simpler to build, it often results in lower labor and material costs. Modern ADUs can still look stylish and welcoming while keeping the overall project affordable and easier to permit. Whether you choose a traditional or modern aesthetic, understanding the cost implications helps you make a choice that aligns with your budget, your goals, and the look you want for your property.

## The Importance of a Detailed "Design Brief"

Before you meet with any architect, designer, or engineer, it is essential to create a Design Brief—a simple but powerful document that clearly explains what you want from your ADU project. Think of it as your project's mission statement. It guides your professional team, keeps the design process focused, and helps prevent misunderstandings that could lead to extra costs or unnecessary revisions. A strong Design Brief should include the following:

1. Project Goals: Clearly state the main purpose of your ADU. Is your top priority generating rental income? Providing a safe and comfortable home for an aging parent? Creating a quiet workspace? Defining this early helps your design team make smart decisions that support your long-term plans.
2. Budget Target: Give your team a realistic budget for construction—not including and or "soft costs" like permits and design fees. Professionals can only design within your financial limits if they understand them. A clear budget prevents them from proposing layouts or features you cannot afford.
3. Must-Haves: These are the non-negotiable features your ADU must include for the project to be successful. This could be the number of bedrooms, accessibility needs, storage requirements, a full-size washer and dryer, or anything else essential to the ADU's purpose.
4. Nice-to-Haves: These are optional features you would like but can live without if the budget gets tight—things

like skylights, a deck, high-end finishes, or extra built-ins. Listing these separately helps your team prioritize what matters most. Presenting a clear, organized Design Brief to your professional team ensures they understand your vision from day one. This saves time, reduces costly revisions, and ensures the final plans truly support your needs, your budget, and your goals.

CHAPTER 2

# HIRING YOUR DESIGN & ENGINEERING TEAM

In the Design-Driven DIY model, the most important investment you will make is not lumber, fixtures, or even contractors—it is your design and engineering team. These professionals form the intellectual backbone of your ADU project. Their expertise shapes every detail of the plans you will eventually build from, and those plans are what make it possible for you, as the homeowner, to confidently manage the construction process yourself. Choosing the right team is not about finding the lowest price. In fact, selecting a bargain designer or engineer often leads to incomplete drawings, confusing layouts, or plans that get repeatedly rejected by the city—problems that can cost far more in the long run. What you need are seasoned professionals who understand ADU laws, knowhow to navigate local building codes, and have a proven track record of creating plans that pass plan check on the first try. When your design and engineering team does their job well, the construction phase becomes dramatically simpler. Their detailed, code-compliant plans remove guesswork, reduce the risk of expensive mistakes, and allow you to coordinate trades (electricians, plumbers, framers, etc.) with confidence. Clear plans lead to clear pricing, clear scheduling, and a smoother build overall. In short, investing in an experienced, capable design and engineering team is the foundation of your entire project. They do not just draw your ADU—

they make the DIY pathway possible.

## Architect vs. Designer vs. Drafter: Who You Actually Need

When you start looking for someone to draw your ADU plans, you will quickly discover that the word "designer" can mean several different things. Not all design professionals offer the same level of service, and not all are necessary for every project. Understanding the differences will help you hire the right person while staying within your budget.

- **Architect**: An architect is a fully licensed professional trained to handle the most complex design challenges. They can solve difficult zoning issues, create highly customized designs, and offer full-service project management if needed. Because of their advanced training and licensure, they tend to be the most expensive option. Architects are a great fit for projects that require unique design solutions, complicated site conditions, or a very high level of customization. Building Designer / Draftsperson: These professionals focus on residential structures and are often the best value for ADU projects. They can create high- quality, code-compliant plans at a more affordable price compared to architects. For the majority of ADUs—especially straightforward or standard designs—a skilled building designer or draftsperson is completely sufficient. They understand local codes, can coordinate with engineers, and provide clear plans that pass city approval.

- **Pre-Approved Plan Provider:** Some cities in Southern California offer pre-approved ADU plans that homeowners can use for a quick and inexpensive start. These plans have already been reviewed and accepted by the city, which can reduce time and uncertainty during permitting. However, the biggest trade-off is flexibility—these designs cannot be customized beyond very minor adjustments. If your site has unique conditions or you need a special layout, this option may not work. But if speed and cost are your top priorities, pre-approved plans can be an excellent solution. Choosing the right professional depends on your project's complexity, your budget, and how much customization you need. Understanding these roles helps you invest wisely and avoid paying for services you do not actually require.

## The Value of ADU-Specialized Firms

Building an ADU in Southern California is not the same as building one in any other part of the country. This region has its own set of rules, including strict seismic (earthquake) standards, complex building codes, and energy-efficiency requirements known as Title 24. Because of this, hiring a design firm that specializes specifically in ADUs—and ideally one that works regularly in your county—can make a huge difference in the success of your project. An ADU-focused firm already understands the unique challenges of your area. They know how local planning departments operate, what kinds of plan check comments they frequently issue, and which design solutions are the most cost-effective while still meeting code.

This inside knowledge means fewer surprises, fewer revisions, and a smoother permitting experience.

Experienced ADU specialists also know how to design in a way that makes construction easier and more affordable. They understand the common pitfalls that slow down projects and can help you avoid them from the very beginning. The result is a set of plans that not only passes plan check faster but is also more practical and straightforward to build from. In short, an ADU-specialized firm saves you time, reduces frustration, and increases the chances that your project will stay on budget—all while ensuring your design meets the strict requirements of your specific region.

## Contract Essentials: Protecting Your Investment

Before you sign any agreement with a designer, architect, or engineer, it is crucial to make sure the contract is clear, detailed, and protects your interests. A well-written contract ensures that everyone understands what is included, what is not, and how much it will cost. Start by checking their license on the appropriate California state board website, such as the California Architects Board or the Board for Professional Engineers, Land Surveyors, and Geologists. These databases confirm whether the professional is properly licensed, in good standing, and legally allowed to work on your project. Next, ask for references from at least three recent ADU clients. It is important that the references are for ADUs—not general home remodels or unrelated projects—because ADUs have unique requirements and challenges. When you contact the references, ask specific, targeted questions that reveal how the designer performed during real projects, such as: "How many revisions did it take to get the plans right?" Too many revisions can indicate inexperience or sloppy work. "Did the plans pass the city's plan check on the first submission?" First-pass approval is a strong sign of a skilled and knowledgeable professional. "Were the plans easy for your builder to follow?" Clear, detailed plans reduce confusion, avoid mistakes, and keep construction moving smoothly. A truly great design team provides plans that are so accurate, clear, and thoughtfully prepared that they act almost like a project manager on paper. When the plans are well done, your job as the owner-builder becomes dramatically easier, and the entire construction process becomes far less stressful.

CHAPTER 3

# STRUCTURAL ENGINEERING: THE BLUEPRINT FOR DIY SUCCESS

## Structural Engineering: Your Most Critical Partnership

When you take the Design-Driven DIY approach, one professional becomes absolutely central to the success of your entire ADU project: the structural engineer. Think of this person as the "safety architect" of your building. While the designer focuses on how your ADU looks and functions, the engineer focuses on how it stands up, stays strong, and stays legal. Their work is not optional; it is required by California law. The engineer's drawings provide the exact instructions for how the ADU must be built so it can handle earthquakes, heavy loads, and the specific soil conditions in Southern California. These plans determine things like how deep the foundation must be, what type of wood the walls need, and the exact hardware that keeps the structure from moving during seismic activity. On the construction site, the engineer's plans outrank everything else. If there is ever a question, confusion, or conflict between documents, the structural drawings are the final authority. Your subcontractors—concrete, framing, carpentry—must follow them exactly, down to the size of each bolt and the spacing of each nail. As the owner-builder, you do not need to be an engineer, but you do need to understand the basics of what you are looking at. When you can confidently read the engineer's notes, symbols, and diagrams, you become far more effective at overseeing your ADU project. You will be able to: Communicate clearly with subcontractors. Catch mistakes before they become expensive. Ensure the work matches the legal requirements. Pass inspections with fewer surprises. In this model, the structural engineer is not just another consultant—they are your most important technical partner. Their plans are the roadmap that guides your entire build, helping you complete your ADU safely, correctly, and with confidence.

## Why a Structural Engineer Is Non-Negotiable

If you are building an ADU in California, hiring a structural engineer is not just a smart idea—it is the law. California is one of the most earthquake-prone places in the United States, and the state's building codes are designed to protect homes from serious damage during seismic activity. Because of this, every new ADU must include engineering that shows exactly how the building will stay strong and safe when the ground moves. A structural engineer is the person who designs the foundation, the framing, and all the elements that help the building resist sideways shaking—things like shear walls, hold-downs, and specific metal connectors. These structural pieces are what keep your ADU standing during an earthquake. If you try to submit plans without an engineer's official stamp, the building department will reject the application immediately. Not only is it illegal to build without proper engineering, but it also puts your investment—and anyone inside the ADU—at serious risk. Beyond legal requirements, here is what a professional engineer actually protects you from:

- Foundation issues caused by shifting or weak soil.
- Structural failure during an earthquake.
- Framing mistakes that lead to sagging roofs or cracking walls.
- Long-term damage that lowers the value of your property.
- Unexpected repair costs because the structure was not designed correctly.

In short, a qualified structural engineer ensures your ADU is built to today's safety standards and can handle the real-world conditions of Southern California. They are your first line of defense between a well-built ADU and a construction disaster.

## Reading the Plans: The DIYer's Guide

For most first-time builders, structural plans can feel overwhelming. They are full of symbols, measurements, and notes that look more like a foreign language than a blueprint of your future ADU. But once you understand the basics, you will see that these plans are simply step-by-step instructions for how your unit will be built. Think of structural plans the same way you would think of IKEA instructions—except instead of assembling furniture, you are assembling a building. Your job is not to do the technical work yourself, but to understand what the professionals are doing so you can manage the project with confidence. Here are the three most important parts of the structural drawings, explained in simple, everyday language:

1. Foundation Details: The "Feet" of Your ADU The foun-

dation is what your entire ADU sits on, and the engineer will show you exactly how it must be built. When looking at this section of the plans, you will see information such as: Footing Sizes (Depth and Width): These are the trenches or pads that get filled with concrete. They are like thick, sturdy "shoes" that keep the ADU stable and prevent sinking or shifting. Rebar Schedule: Rebar refers to the metal bars placed inside the concrete to make it stronger. The plans will show what size the bars should be, how many are needed, and how far apart they must be. This helps your concrete crew know exactly how to build a strong, code-approved foundation. Anchor Bolts: These bolts connect the wooden structure to the concrete slab. Think of them as the screws that keep the building "attached to the ground," especially during earthquakes. If the foundation is wrong, nothing else can be right, which is why these details matter so much.

2. Shear Wall Details: The "Muscles" That Keep the ADU Safe in Earthquakes in California, one of the biggest jobs of a building is to stay standing during an earthquake. That is where shear walls come in. They keep the structure from swaying or collapsing when the ground moves. On the plans, you will find: Where the Shear Walls Are Located: These walls look like regular walls but are built stronger. The plans mark exactly which walls need extra support. Type of Sheathing (Plywood or OSB): This is the wood paneling attached to the framing. The engineer will specify the type of wood, the thickness, and which sides of the wall to install it on. Nailing Pattern: This tells the framer how many nails to use, what size they should be, and how far apart they should be. California's building code is very specific about this because it determines how

well the wall stands up to earthquake forces. Metal Connectors (Simpson Ties): These are small but powerful pieces of hardware that reinforce the structure. They keep everything "locked together" so the ADU acts like one solid piece. Shear wall plans are basically the earthquake safety map for your framing crew.

3. Load-Bearing Points: How the Weight Travels Down to the Ground Every part of your ADU—roof, ceilings, walls—has weight. The structural plans show how that weight safely travels down to the foundation. This part of the plans tells you: Where the Big Loads Are Located: These are areas where extra support is needed, such as under the roof, over large window openings, or under long spans of ceiling. Beams and Headers: These are heavy-duty pieces of wood or engineered lumber that hold up the weight of the structure. The plans show exactly what type of beam to use, how big it should be, and what it is made of (regular lumber, LVL, glulam, etc.). Whenever you see a large opening like a big window or sliding door, a beam or header is carrying the weight above it. The structural plans make this extremely clear, so the framers know what to install.

## The Engineer's Role in Simplifying the Build

One of the biggest advantages of working with an experienced structural engineer— especially one who understands that you are building your ADU as a DIY owner-builder —is that they will design your project in a way that is simple, practical, and cost- effective. Good engineering does not just make your ADU safe; it also saves you time, money, and stress during construction. A thoughtful engineer will always aim to create a structure that is strong without being complicated and efficient without being expensive. Here is how they do it: Standardizing Materials (Making the Build Easier for You): A skilled engineer knows that DIY builders and small crews work more efficiently when the materials are familiar and easy to find. Instead of calling for unusual or custom elements, they will use common lumber sizes (such as 2x4s, 2x6s, and standard beams), specify widely available hardware from brands like Simpson Strong-Tie, and avoid specialty products that require special ordering. This approach reduces confusion for your subcontractors and helps you avoid unnecessary trips to the lumber yard. Optimizing for Cost (Strong but Not Overbuilt): In construction, "over- engineering" can happen when the plans call for beams, hardware, or foundations that are stronger—and more expensive—than necessary. A good engineer avoids this by designing only what is needed to meet code and keep the ADU safe. This means they work to use the smallest and most affordable materials that still meet safety requirements, reduce unnecessary metal connectors, and keep the structural system as straightforward as possible for your crew to build. The result? A structure that is safe, stable, and legal, without blowing your budget on materials you do not actually need. In short, when your structural engineer understands the goals of the Design-Driven DIY approach, they become a true partner. They help you build an ADU that is easier to construct, cheaper to build, and simpler to manage—all while remaining fully safe and code-compliant. Great engineering is not just about safety; it is about making your entire project run smoother from day one.

# PART II

## BRINGING IN THE PROS

CHAPTER 4

# HIRING THE RIGHT GC FOR THE BIG 3

On two different backyard ADU projects, the homeowners made two very different choices.

- **Homeowner A** hired the cheapest GC they could find for "everything." The bid was vague, the schedule slipped, inspections kept failing, and the owner felt pressured into expensive change orders. By the time the shell was finished, the budget was shredded, and trust was gone.
- **Homeowner B** hired a GC with one clear job: **build a straight, safe, code-compliant shell**—the Big 3. They agreed on a fixed price for site prep, foundation, and framing, tied payments to passed inspections, and then the GC stepped away. The homeowner took over finishes with a clean, inspected structure and a clear budget.

Same method—Design-Driven DIY. Completely different experience.

In this chapter, we'll focus on one powerful option inside the Design-Driven DIY approach:

*Hiring a General Contractor (GC) just for the Big 3—site prep, foundation, and framing—then taking over once you have a safe, inspected shell.*

You can absolutely choose to hire separate foundation and framing crews instead of a GC. But if you decide to bring in a GC for structure, the way you **select, vet, and contract with them** will largely determine whether your project feels smooth and controlled—or chaotic and expensive.

By the end of this chapter, you'll know how to:

- Find Hybrid-friendly contractors who accept Big 3–only scopes
- Filter them with a step-by-step vetting process
- Lock in a contract that protects your budget and supports your Design-Driven DIY plan

## Why the Big 3 GC Matters So Much

Your GC for the Big 3 is the person responsible for the structural backbone of your ADU:

- Shaping and preparing your site
- Building the foundation your engineer designed
- Framing the shell that everything else depends on

When you choose well, a good GC will:

- Deliver a straight, solid, code-compliant shell
- Keep inspections smooth and organized
- Protect you from costly structural mistakes
- Stay on schedule and within the agreed scope

A bad GC will:

- Blow through your budget with change orders and "surprises"
- Fail inspections and blame everyone else
- Cause conflicts with subs, inspectors, and neighbors
- Leave you with a crooked, problem-prone structure you'll fight for years

In a Design-Driven DIY build, you **never DIY the Big 3**—but that doesn't mean anyone can do them. This chapter is about finding someone who understands and respects your plan: **pros handle structure; you handle finishes.**

## Finding a "Hybrid-Friendly" Contractor

In this book, I'll keep using "***Hybrid***" as shorthand for this idea:

You hire a GC for the Big 3 only, then take over as owner-builder for everything after the shell is complete.

Not every contractor likes this. Many GCs want to run the entire job from excavation to final paint. If you bring that person into a Hybrid scope, they may fight you, upsell you, or quietly sabotage your plan.

You're looking for a GC who:

- Respects your role as owner-builder
- Is comfortable with a clearly defined, Big 3–only scope
- Has actually done shell-only or phase-1 projects before
- Doesn't try to pressure you into giving them "the whole job"

Here are your best sources.

## *1. Referrals from Architects & Designers*

This is the **gold standard.**

Why it's powerful:

- Architects and designers want their projects built correctly
- They remember who follows plans carefully
- They steer away from contractors who create headaches or ignore details

When you talk to your designer or architect, ask:

"Who are your top 2–3 contractors for ADU shell or framing-only work? Ideally people you trust to follow your plans exactly on site."

A GC who has already earned a designer's trust is more likely to respect your engineered plans and your Design-Driven DIY strategy.

## *2. ADU-Specialist Companies*

Many ADU-focused companies:

- Understand local ADU codes and typical plan-check issues
- Already offer "shell-only," "Phase 1," or "core & shell" packages
- Know the inspectors and permitting staff in your area
- Have internal systems built around standardized, repeatable structural work

Because they work on ADUs all the time, these companies are often more open to **Hybrid workflows**—they've seen owner-builders take over after the shell and understand where the handoff happens.

When you find an ADU specialist, ask directly:

"Do you offer a shell-only or Phase 1 package where you just handle site prep, foundation, and framing?"

If the answer is "Yes, we do that all the time," you're in the right conversation.

### *3. Targeted Online Searches*

If referrals are limited, you can still find candidates online. Search with phrases like:

- "ADU shell contractor [your city]"
- "ADU framing contractor [your county]"
- "foundation and framing ADU [city]"
- "detached garage framing [city]"

You're looking for:

- Clear photos of foundations, framing, and structural work
- Multiple ADU, garage, or small detached projects—not just kitchen remodels
- Mentions of ADUs, accessory buildings, or detached structures in their copy

Then, you'll filter for Hybrid-friendliness in conversation.

## Early Warning Signs They're *Not* Hybrid-Friendly

Walk away—or at least be very cautious—if you hear things like:

- "You have to hire me for everything, not just the shell."
- "Owner-builders always mess things up."
- "I don't really do ADUs, but construction is construction."

You want a partner in your Design-Driven DIY plan, not a reluctant babysitter who resents your involvement.

### *The Vetting Process: Step-by-Step*

Great GCs aren't "found" through gut feeling. They're filtered through a simple, disciplined process.

Once you've built a shortlist, move each candidate through the same funnel:

1. Verify license and insurance
2. Check ADU-relevant references
3. Review their portfolio
4. Get a detailed, itemized bid

Only then do you talk seriously about contracts and schedules.

### *Step 1: Verify License & Insurance*

***This is non-negotiable.***

For California, use the CSLB (Contractors State License Board) website to confirm:

- Their license is active and correctly classified (typically a B – General Building Contractor)
- They carry general liability insurance
- They have workers' compensation insurance if they have employees

If anything here is unclear or missing, cross them off your list. No exceptions.

This step alone will eliminate a surprising number of risky candidates.

### *Step 2: Check ADU-Relevant References*

Ask for **at least 3–5 recent projects** similar to yours:

- Detached ADUs
- Garage conversions
- Small detached structures

When you call references, ask specific questions:

- "Did the final cost stay close to the original bid?"
- "How many change orders were there—and what caused them?"
- "How did inspections go—smoothly, or were there repeated failures?"
- "Were they respectful of your property and neighbors?"
- "Would you hire them again for a similar project?"

You're looking for patterns, not perfection. One rough project in ten is human. Three rough projects in a row is a huge red flag.

## Step 3: Review Their Portfolio

Ask to see:

- Photos of foundations, framing, and site work
- Any ADUs or small detached buildings they've completed
- Jobs in your city or neighboring jurisdictions

You're checking that:

- Their framing is straight, plumb, and not chaotic
- They've handled sloped or tight lots if your site is similar
- Job sites look organized and safe, not like a junkyard

If all their photos are of kitchens and bathrooms and they can't show structural work, they might not be the right fit for the Big 3.

## Step 4: Get a Detailed, Itemized Bid

A solid GC bid for the Big 3 should:

- Break down labor and materials for each phase:
    - Site prep
    - Foundation
    - Framing & shear walls
    - Roof sheathing and basic weatherproofing (if included)
- Clearly show what is and is not included

- Reference your actual engineered plans, not generic "ballpark" numbers

Red flags:

- One-line "lump sum" for "ADU build"
- Bids dramatically lower than the others without a good explanation
- Vague language like "misc. items as needed" with no detail

Remember:

*You're comparing scope, not just numbers. A low bid that quietly omits key work (house wrap, hardware, drainage, etc.) is not really cheaper.*

## The "3-Bid Reality Check"

When possible, get at least **three bids** on the same plan set and written Big 3 scope.

Most of the time:

- One will be clearly too high
- One will be suspiciously low
- One will be in the middle and best aligned with reality

That "middle" bid is often your strongest candidate—if:

- They passed your license and reference checks
- Their scope matches what you need
- You trust them after conversation

Don't pick a GC just because they're the cheapest. Pick the

one who is most likely to build your structural shell correctly and predictably.

## The Contract: Your Legal Safety Net

The contract you sign with your GC is more important than any handshake, promise, or "don't worry, we'll take care of you."

Your contract should:

- Support your Hybrid / Design-Driven DIY plan
- Lock in a clear scope (Big 3 only)
- Tie payments to objective milestones
- Define how changes, delays, and inspections will be handled

Let's walk through the essentials.

### *1. Fixed Price for the Big 3*

You want a fixed-price contract that covers:

- Site preparation (grading, excavation, trenching as agreed)
- Foundation (formed and poured per engineering)
- Framing (walls, floors, roof, shear walls, hardware)
- All associated inspections for these phases

This keeps your structural work predictable and prevents slow "price creep."

Most GCs will still exclude true unknowns (like hitting unexpected rock or buried debris) from fixed pricing—that's normal. The goal is to make everything else as fixed and clear as possible.

### 2. Clear Scope of Work

Spell out exactly what the GC is responsible for, such as:

- Grading and excavation (within defined limits)
- Utility trenching (if included)
- Forming and pouring the foundation
- Anchor bolts, hold-downs, and structural hardware installation
- Framing walls, floors, and roof according to engineered plans
- Sheathing, housewrap, and basic weatherproofing (if included)
- Scheduling and coordinating inspections for their scope

Also spell out what they are not doing:

- No insulation, drywall, painting
- No interior finishes or trim
- No cabinet or fixture installation
- No landscaping, fencing, or hardscape (unless specifically added)
- No management of your later subs or finishes

A clear scope prevents "But I thought that was included..." arguments and keeps your Hybrid plan intact.

### 3. Payment Schedule Tied to Milestones

Structure payments based on completed work, not time

alone. For example:

- Small deposit (e.g., 10%) once permits are ready and start date is set
- Payment after inspection-approved foundation
- Payment after framing & shear wall inspection passes
- Payment after roof sheathing and weatherproofing (if included) pass inspection
- Final payment only after a brief punch list of Big 3 items is complete

Avoid front-loading payments. You always want the contractor slightly ahead in work, not ahead in money.

For each payment, require:

- **Conditional lien releases** with invoices
- **Unconditional lien releases** after payment clears

This protects you from future claims by the GC or their subs.

### *4. Change Order Process*

Your contract should clearly describe:

- **What counts as a change order** (scope changes, owner-requested upgrades, unforeseen conditions)
- **How costs are calculated** (fixed fee per item, labor + materials with a markup, etc.)
- **How change orders must be approved** (in writing, by you, before work proceeds)

This prevents "Oh, that was an extra $5,000" conversations after the fact.

Make it clear:

> *No work outside the written scope is authorized without a signed change order.*

### *5. Timeline, Delays & Responsibilities*

The agreement should include:

- Estimated start and completion dates for the Big 3
- How weather delays, material delays, or inspection delays are handled
- How long the GC can pause the project without cause
- Who is responsible for:
    - Scheduling inspections
    - Communicating with inspectors
    - Site safety, fencing, and signage
    - Daily cleanup and debris removal
    - Protecting existing structures, fences, and landscaping

In some markets, it may also make sense to discuss schedule incentives or penalties—but even a clearly written timeline is a huge step up from "we'll get to it when we get to it."

## When to Bring in an Attorney

It's worth having a construction-savvy attorney review your contract if:

- The contract value is large relative to your savings and

risk tolerance

- The GC is providing their own complex, multi-page contract
- You're unsure about any clause, exclusion, or guarantee

Spending a little on legal review up front can prevent massive headaches later.

## Chapter Checklist (Quick Review)

Before moving on, you should be able to say "yes" to all of these:

- ☐ I understand how hiring a GC for the Big 3 fits into the Design-Driven DIY method
- ☐ I know where to look for Hybrid-friendly GCs or ADU specialists
- ☐ I know how to verify license and insurance through CSLB
- ☐ I have a list of specific questions to ask references
- ☐ I know what a detailed, itemized Big 3 bid should include
- ☐ I understand the key elements my GC contract must cover
- ☐ I know how the contract protects my Hybrid plan and Big 3 scope

## Action Steps

1. Create a shortlist of 3–6 potential GCs using referrals from your designer and targeted online searches.

2. Verify each candidate's license and insurance through CSLB (or your state's equivalent).
3. Request itemized bids based on your actual engineered plans and a written Big 3 scope.
4. Ask each GC for 3–5 ADU or similar project references and schedule quick calls.
5. Draft a one-page "Big 3 Scope Summary":
   - What they will do
   - What they will not do
   - Where their responsibility ends and your owner-builder role begins
6. Attach this scope summary to your contract and confirm that both the bid and contract match it.

You now have the framework to choose a GC who can build your ADU's structural shell without taking over your entire project.

## Scripts & Questions You Can Use

Use or adapt these scripts to keep conversations clear and aligned with your Hybrid plan.

### *Script: Initial Call with a GC*

*"Hi, I'm building an ADU and following a design-first, owner-managed approach. I'm looking for a General Contractor to handle only the Big 3: site work, foundation, and framing, based on engineered plans. Is that a scope you're comfortable with, and have you done ADU shell-only or phase-1 projects before?"*

### *Script: Asking for References*

*"Before we move forward, could you send me contact info for three recent ADU or small-structure clients—ideally projects similar in size to mine—so I can ask them about their experience with your foundation and framing work?"*

### *Questions to Ask References*

- "Did the final price stay close to the original bid?"
- "How did inspections go—smoothly, or were there repeated failures?"
- "Were you happy with the quality and straightness of the foundation and framing?"
- "How did they handle schedule delays or surprises?"
- "Would you hire them again for a similar project?"

### *Script: Clarifying Scope with the GC*

*"I'll be taking over after the shell is complete as an owner-builder. Can we walk through the plans and create a written list of exactly what you'll deliver by the end of your scope—so we both know where your work stops and mine begins?"*

### *Self-Check Questions Before Signing*

- "Do I trust this GC to build the structural backbone of my ADU?"
- "Do I clearly understand what's included in the price—and what isn't?"
- "Does this contract support my Hybrid plan, or quietly lock me into more than I want?"

- "If this GC walked away after the Big 3, would I feel confident taking over from there?"

If you can answer "yes" to those questions—on paper and in your gut—you're ready to move forward.

In the next chapter, we'll zoom in on structural engineering and inspections from your side of the table, so you know what your GC and engineer are doing, what inspectors are looking for, and how to keep the Big 3 phases moving without surprises.

CHAPTER 5

# SITE PREP ESSENTIALS (GRADING, TRENCHING, SEWER, POWER)

On paper, "site prep" looks simple: scrape some dirt, dig some trenches, move on. In real life, I've watched more ADU projects stall or spiral here than at any other phase.

- One homeowner's GC rushed trenching and backfilled before inspection. The city flagged the work, the crew had to re-excavate, and they lost three weeks plus thousands of dollars.
- Another homeowner took time to walk the site with their GC, confirm drainage paths, and photograph every trench before backfill. Their inspections passed on the first try, and their foundation started on schedule.

Same soil, same city. The difference was **how seriously they treated site prep.**

*Nearly every ADU delay I've seen traces back to site prep—something missed, rushed, or misunderstood before concrete was ever poured.*

In the Design-Driven DIY model, you're not out there running machines or laying pipe. But you are responsible for understanding what's happening and making sure it matches the plans.

This chapter will show you:

- What "site prep" actually includes
- Why it's riskier than it looks
- How to oversee this phase without micromanaging
- The most common mistakes—and how to avoid them

By the end, you'll know how to watch this phase like a pro, without ever touching a shovel.

## Why This Phase Matters So Much

Site preparation is not glamorous. There's no pretty tile, no paint colors, no cabinets. Just dirt, trenches, and inspections.

But it's foundational in the truest sense:

- It determines how water moves around (and away from) your ADU
- It sets up the building pad your foundation relies on
- It places the underground utilities your ADU will use for decades
- It's where inspectors first interact with your project

When site prep goes wrong, you can end up with:

- Drainage problems that never fully go away
- Failed inspections before the foundation even begins
- Expensive rework after utilities are installed
- Conflicts between trades later in construction

Done correctly, site prep makes everything that follows—foundation, framing, utilities, inspections—move faster and with far fewer surprises.

## What Site Prep Actually Includes

> *Professional site prep crews think three steps ahead—because fixing mistakes later is always harder.*

Site preparation transforms your yard into a construction-ready platform. Your GC or site-work contractor handles the tools and labor, but you should understand the major steps and what they're trying to achieve.

At a high level, site prep includes:

1. Demolition & clearing
2. Grading
3. Trenching for utilities
4. Utility rough-ins and inspections

Let's walk through each.

### *1. Demolition & Clearing*

This first step removes anything in the way of your building pad and trenches. It may include:

- Removing sheds, old slabs, or patios
- Clearing vegetation, roots, and stumps
- Hauling away debris and unusable material
- Fencing or securing the work area for safety

Why it matters:

- Hidden debris, concrete chunks, or roots can interfere with grading and compaction.
- Leftover roots can rot and cause settlement under your future foundation.
- A clean, fenced site keeps the work safer and helps inspectors take your project seriously.

## *2. Grading*

Grading reshapes the land so that:

- The building pad is reasonably level and ready for foundation forms
- Water drains away from the future foundation and structures
- Soil is compacted to support structural loads and prevent settlement

Good grading:

- Protects your ADU from moisture intrusion
- Reduces the risk of standing water or erosion
- Makes forming and pouring the foundation simpler and more accurate

This is where your site plan meets reality. The goal is to give your foundation crew a stable, well-drained starting point.

## *3. Trenching for Utilities*

Once the general shape of the site is set, crews dig trenches for the services your ADU needs:

- Sewer
- Water
- Electrical
- Gas (if applicable)

These trenches must follow your approved plans and local code:

- Depths must meet minimum requirements for frost protection and safety
- Sewer lines must maintain proper slope toward the connection point
- Routing must avoid existing utilities, tree roots, and restricted easements

Poor trenching is one of the fastest ways to fail inspections. It's not enough to "just get a pipe in the ground"—it has to be in the right place, at the right depth, with the right slope.

### *4. Utility Rough-Ins*

Once trenches are open, crews install the infrastructure your ADU will use for decades:

- Pipes and conduits are placed in the trenches
- Connections are made to the main house or street, as shown on your plans
- Cleanouts, shutoffs, and access points are installed in accessible locations
- Everything is inspected before backfill

Think of this as installing the veins and arteries of your ADU. You won't see most of this work once it's buried, but you'll depend on it every time you flush a toilet, turn on a light, or take a shower.

## Why Site Prep Is High-Risk (Even Though It Looks Simple)

Site prep feels deceptively basic: dirt in, dirt out, trenches in between.

But:

- Most work happens underground
- Errors are hard to see once buried
- Fixes often require re-excavation of finished areas
- Inspections happen early—and failures stop the project cold

This is why attention now prevents disasters later. If you're going to be picky anywhere, be picky about:

- Drainage
- Trench placement and depth
- Inspection timing

## How to Oversee Site Prep (Without Micromanaging)

The best owner-builders don't interfere—they observe intelligently.

You don't need to tell crews how to dig or grade. Your job is to:

- Make sure work lines up with plans and intent
- Ask clear questions when something seems off
- Protect your future self by documenting what's being

buried

Think of yourself as a second set of eyes, not a replacement supervisor.

**Here's what to pay attention to.**

## 1. Drainage Direction

Confirm that:

- The ground slopes away from the future foundation area
- There are no obvious low spots where water will collect near the building pad
- Downspouts and surface drainage have a clear path away from structures

Poor drainage is one of the most common long-term ADU problems. It's much easier to fix with a skid steer now than with French drains and sump pumps later.

## 2. Trench Depth & Placement

Ask (and verify) that:

- Trenches match the depths and locations shown on the plans
- Sewer lines have the proper slope from the ADU to the connection point
- Water and electrical trenches are at code-compliant depths and separated as required
- Trenches don't cross areas they shouldn't (roots, existing foundations, property lines)

If you're unsure, it's perfectly reasonable to say:

***"Can you show me on the plans where this trench is supposed to run, and what depth you're targeting?"***

Shallow or misplaced trenches almost always fail inspection—and re-digging trenches is no one's favorite job.

### *3. Protection of Existing Structures*

Watch for how your GC or site crew treats what you already have:

- Are they avoiding damage to your main house foundation?
- Are walkways, patios, and driveways being protected as much as possible?
- Are visible utility lines clearly marked and avoided?
- Are significant tree roots near critical areas being handled thoughtfully (or with an arborist, if needed)?

Good contractors protect what's already there. If you see casual damage brushed off as "normal," that's a red flag for how they may treat your entire project.

### *Red Flags During Site Prep*

Pay attention if you see any of the following:

- Trenches dug without referencing plans
- Backfilling before inspection approval
- Standing water near the building pad after grading
- No clear utility shutoffs identified for new connections
- Damage to existing structures or utilities dismissed as "no big deal"

Any of these deserve immediate questions. You don't need to be confrontational—just calmly ask what's going on and how they plan to address it.

## Common Site Prep Mistakes (and How to Avoid Them)

A few problems show up again and again in ADU projects:

1. Rushing to pour concrete before utilities are inspected
   - Fix: Make sure your GC confirms all required inspections are passed before backfill or forms go in.
2. Assuming old sewer lines are usable without verification
   - Fix: Ask whether existing lines have been camera-inspected or pressure-tested before connecting your ADU.
3. Ignoring drainage because "it's dry most of the year"
   - Fix: Design and verify a clear drainage plan now. Water always shows up eventually.
4. Letting trenches be backfilled too early
   - Fix: Confirm inspection sign-offs (or photos plus inspector approval) before any trench is closed.
5. Not documenting underground work
   - Fix: Take clear photos of every trench, connection, and cleanout before it's buried. Your future self—and future plumbers—will thank you.

Site prep rewards patience and planning. The more you slow down now, the less you'll be forced to slow down later.

## Chapter Checklist (Quick Review)

Before moving on, make sure you can say "yes" to:

- I understand the purpose of site prep and how it fits into the Big 3
- I know what demolition, grading, trenching, and utility rough-ins include
- I know what to watch for during grading and trenching (drainage, depth, placement)
- I understand why inspections happen before backfill and how they affect the schedule
- I know which site prep mistakes cause the biggest delays and rework
- I feel confident overseeing—not managing—this stage as an informed owner-builder

## Action Steps (Do These Before Site Work Begins)

Take 20–30 minutes to prepare for site prep:

1. Review the site plan and utility layouts carefully.Make sure you can roughly trace where sewer, water, power, and gas will run.
2. Walk the yard and visualize trench routes. Note trees, roots, existing patios, and anything that might be affected.
3. Identify existing utilities and shutoff points. Know where your current water, gas, and electrical shutoffs are located.
4. Ask your GC to explain the inspection sequence.

"Which inspections happen during site prep, and in what order? What has to be exposed for each?"

5. Plan to take photos of trenches before backfill. Create a folder on your phone or in your ADU binder labeled "Underground Utilities."

These steps will make you a calmer, more effective observer when the machines roll in.

## Scripts & Questions You Can Use

Use these to keep communication clear and confident.

### *Script: Before Site Work Starts*

*"Before you start grading and trenching, can we walk the site together? I'd like to understand how drainage will move away from the ADU and where the main utility trenches will run."*

### *Script: During Trenching*

*"Before any trenches are backfilled, can we confirm that all required inspections are scheduled and approved—and that I can take a few photos for my records?"*

### *Questions to Ask Your GC or Site Crew*

- "How do you confirm proper sewer slope before inspection?"
- "Where are the cleanouts and shutoffs located for the ADU?"
- "What happens if an inspector asks for changes at this stage?"

- "Are any existing utilities or structures at risk during this work?"
- "If something unexpected is found underground, how will you handle pricing and communication?"

### *Self-Check Questions*

As site prep progresses, periodically ask yourself:

- "Do trench locations match the approved plans and the general layout I was shown?"
- "Has anything been buried that I didn't see or document?"
- "Would I understand this layout in 5–10 years if a plumber or electrician needed to make repairs?"
- "Do I feel clear on what inspections have happened and what's coming next?"

If the answer to any of these is "no," that's your cue to pause and ask for clarification.

## What Comes Next

Once site prep passes inspection, your project is officially ready for foundation work—the moment when your ADU begins to take physical shape above the ground.

In the next chapter, we'll look at foundations made simple: what your engineer has designed, what your GC and concrete crew are actually doing on site, and how to spot obvious issues before they're locked in forever.

CHAPTER 6

# FOUNDATION TYPES & PICKING THE RIGHT ONE (BEGINNER-FRIENDLY GUIDE)

On two different ADU builds, I watched foundations take two very different paths.

- **Project A** tried to "save money" by pushing the engineer toward a thinner slab and rushing through inspections. Rebar wasn't exactly where it should have been, plumbing stubs were off by a few inches, and the vapor barrier was damaged. The pour went ahead anyway. Within months, hairline cracks appeared, a shower drain was in the wrong place, and doors never quite closed right.
- **Project B** followed the engineered plans exactly. The GC slowed down for rebar and plumbing checks, passed inspections cleanly, and took curing seriously. Years later, the floors are still level, doors swing smoothly, and there are no mystery cracks.

*Same city. Same code. Very different outcomes.*

Across every ADU project I've reviewed, foundation mistakes

are the most expensive—and the hardest to undo.

In the Design-Driven DIY model, the foundation is one of the Big 3 phases you never DIY. But understanding your options and the process will help you choose the right foundation for your property and oversee this critical stage with confidence—before the concrete is poured.

## Why This Phase Matters (Read First)

The foundation is the single most important structural investment in your ADU. Everything else—walls, roof, plumbing, finishes, and long-term value—rests on it.

When a foundation is done right:

- Framing goes faster and straighter
- Inspections pass with fewer comments
- Floors stay level
- Cracks and moisture issues are minimized
- The ADU performs better in earthquakes

When it's done wrong, "fixes" can require:

- Demolition
- Re-engineering
- Partial or complete replacement

This chapter will help you:

- Understand the main foundation types for ADUs
- See how engineers match foundation type to your specific lot
- Follow the step-by-step foundation process
- Know what to check before the pour so you don't lock

in avoidable mistakes

## Why Foundations Matter So Much in Southern California

In seismic zones, the foundation doesn't just hold the building up—it keeps it together.

Think of your foundation as the feet and ankles of your ADU. If they're weak, the entire body suffers.

In Southern California, foundations must:

- Support the full structural load of the building
- Resist earthquake forces and lateral movement
- Accommodate soil movement and moisture conditions
- Meet strict seismic and building codes

That's why foundations are always engineered, not improvised—and why inspections at this stage are especially strict.

### *A Hard Truth About Foundations*

Once concrete is poured, changes are nearly impossible.

> This is the last moment where questions are cheap.

If something feels rushed or unclear, this is the time to slow things down and ask.

## Common Foundation Types for ADUs

The "best" foundation is the one that fits your lot—not the one that's cheapest on paper.

Your structural engineer will recommend a foundation type based on:

- Lot slope
- Soil conditions
- Drainage and groundwater
- ADU design and loads
- Local code requirements
- Budget and constructability

Here are the most common options you'll see.

### *1. Slab-on-Grade Foundation*

Most common. Often most affordable.

A slab-on-grade is a solid concrete slab poured directly on prepared soil, typically over compacted gravel and reinforced with steel.

Why homeowners and builders like it:

- Lowest cost in many cases
- Fastest to construct
- Ideal for flat or gently sloped lots
- Fewer structural components to coordinate

**Important note:**

Plumbing and electrical conduits are often embedded in the slab. That means:

- Drain locations must be correct
- Future changes are difficult or impossible without cutting concrete

Coordination before the pour is critical.

## 2. Raised Foundation (Crawl Space)

A raised foundation lifts the ADU above ground, creating a crawl space underneath.

Good choice if:

- Your lot slopes and you want to avoid major grading
- You want future access to plumbing or some electrical runs
- Moisture or drainage is a concern
- You prefer wood-framed floors instead of concrete underfoot

Trade-off:

- Higher upfront cost than basic slab-on-grade
- Slightly longer construction timeline

But you get:

- Easier long-term maintenance and flexibility
- Better access for repairs, upgrades, or retrofits

### *3. Engineered Foundations (Pier & Beam, Mat Slab, Etc.)*

These systems are used when conditions are more challenging, such as:

- Steep slopes
- Poor or unstable soil
- Tight setbacks or unusual lot shapes
- Higher-than-usual structural loads

Examples include:

- Pier and beam systems
- Mat slabs (thick, heavily reinforced slabs)
- Hybrid systems with grade beams, deepened footings, or special anchoring

These foundations are:

- Custom-designed by a structural engineer
- More expensive than standard slabs or simple raised foundations
- Sometimes the only safe and legal option for certain properties

## When the Engineer Overrides the Budget

If your engineer specifies a complex foundation, it's not optional. They're solving a problem your property already has ignoring it doesn't make that problem go away.

It can be frustrating when the "simple slab" you imagined becomes a more expensive system. But that extra cost is buying you safety, code compliance, and long-term stability.

## The Foundation Process: Step-by-Step

Owner-builders don't manage foundations—they verify readiness. You won't be tying rebar or setting forms, but understanding the sequence will help you spot issues before they're buried forever.

Here's what typically happens.

### *1. Formwork (Creating the Mold)*

Carpenters build wood forms to shape the foundation exactly as drawn on the plans.

You should see:

- Dimensions that match the engineering drawings
- Straight, square, and stable forms
- Correct thickness and depth where footings are called out

If you walk the site and something looks obviously crooked or the footprint seems off, that's worth a conversation before concrete shows up.

### *2. Rebar & Steel Reinforcement*

Concrete is strong in compression but weak in tension. That's why it needs steel.

This step includes:

- Rebar placed in exact locations per the engineering
- Specific bar sizes and spacing
- Proper laps and bends where bars connect

- Secure ties holding bars in position

Inspectors pay close attention here because:

- This steel will soon be invisible
- It's critical for seismic performance

This is a key moment for you to walk the site with the structural plans in hand and ask your GC:

***"Can you show me how this rebar layout matches the engineering drawings?"***

### *3. Plumbing & Electrical Rough-Ins*

Before concrete is poured, subs install:

- Drain lines (sewer)
- Water lines
- Sleeves or conduits for electrical and, sometimes, low-voltage or gas

These must be installed exactly where the plans show, at the correct depths and slopes.

Mistakes at this stage are extremely expensive to fix later. Fixing a misplaced shower drain or main sewer line often means:

- Cutting the slab
- Jackhammering out concrete
- Re-pouring patched sections

Much better to catch issues now, while everything is open.

### *4. The Concrete Pour*

Once forms, rebar, vapor barrier, and rough-ins pass inspection, it's time to pour.

During the pour:

- Concrete is delivered and placed in a continuous operation
- Crews spread, vibrate, and level the mix
- Edges and surfaces are shaped according to the plans

Here, timing matters:

- Hot, dry, or windy weather can cause rapid drying and cracks
- Cold, wet weather can affect curing and strength

Your GC will schedule the pour for acceptable conditions—or adjust the mix and curing plan accordingly.

### *5. Finishing & Curing*

After pouring:

- The surface is leveled and smoothed (to the specified finish)
- Anchor bolts and hardware are set where required
- The concrete begins to cure over several days

Curing must be controlled:

- Drying too fast can cause shrinkage cracks and reduced strength
- Proper curing (often with moisture retention measures) helps the slab reach its designed performance

Ask your GC how they plan to protect the slab in the first days after the pour.

## Why Foundations Fail Inspections

Common reasons foundations fail inspection include:

- Missing or misplaced rebar
- Incorrect footing depth or width
- No or incomplete vapor barrier
- Plumbing not matching the plans
- Pouring before required inspections are approved

You don't have to be the inspector—but you can double-check that these basics have been addressed before anyone calls for inspection or schedules a concrete truck.

## How to Oversee the Foundation Phase

Your goal is confirmation—not correction.

You're not telling crews how to tie rebar or finish concrete. You are making sure:

- Work matches the structural plans
- Inspections happen in the right order
- Nothing gets rushed "just to keep things moving"

Here's what to check before the pour.

### *Rebar Placement*

Confirm, with your GC or foreman, that rebar:

- Matches the engineering drawings (sizes, spacing, and locations)

- Is tied securely so it won't shift during the pour
- Is elevated off the soil using chairs or supports (not lying directly on dirt)

Take photos of rebar layouts before the inspector arrives and before concrete is placed. If there's ever a question later, you'll have a record.

### *Vapor Barrier (for Slab-on-Grade)*

Look for:

- Plastic sheeting over the soil under the slab area
- Seams overlapped and taped (not gapped)
- Penetrations sealed around pipes and conduits

A good vapor barrier:

- Helps protect flooring from moisture
- Improves indoor air quality
- Reduces long-term condensation and mold risks

### *Inspection Approval*

Nothing should be poured until:

- All required pre-pour inspections are complete
- Approval is clearly confirmed (often via written sign-off or online portal)

**It's okay to ask:**

> *"Have all required inspections passed, and do we have documentation before we schedule or start the pour?"*

If you're not satisfied with the answer, pause and clarify—this is the moment to slow things down.

### *Curing Plan*

Before the pour, ask your GC:

- "How will the concrete be protected from rapid drying?"
- "What curing method will you use (water, curing compound, coverings)?"
- "What weather conditions would cause us to postpone the pour?"

You're not micromanaging; you're making sure there is a plan.

## The One Question That Matters Most

Right before the pour, ask your GC or foreman:

> *"Is there anything we'll wish we double-checked once the concrete is poured?"*

Then stay quiet and let them think. If they mention anything—no matter how small—encourage them to check it now.

## Why Getting the Foundation Right Saves You Money

A good foundation:

- Makes framing easier, faster, and more accurate
- Reduces drywall cracks and door problems later

- Improves energy performance by controlling moisture
- Prevents costly long-term moisture and settlement issues
- Protects resale value and buyer confidence
- Lowers long-term maintenance costs

Foundation mistakes are the most expensive mistakes in construction. Protecting this phase is one of the highest-leverage things you can do as an owner-builder.

## Your Role as the Owner-Builder

Your power at this stage lies in timing, not tools.

During the foundation phase, your responsibilities are to:

- Review structural and foundation plans carefully
- Ask questions early, not the morning of the pour
- Confirm inspections are complete before work moves forward
- Slow the process if something feels rushed or unclear
- Document key stages with photos (rebar, vapor barrier, plumbing, before and after inspections)

Once concrete is poured, your influence ends in this area. Use it wisely before that moment.

## A Quick Review: Chapter Checklist

Before moving on, confirm:

- I understand the main foundation types (slab-on-grade, raised, engineered systems)
- I have a good sense of which one fits my property and

why

- I understand the basic foundation sequence (forms → rebar → rough ins → pour → curing)
- I know what to check before the pour (rebar, vapor barrier, inspections, curing plan)
- I understand why inspections at this stage are critical and strict
- I know my role: observe, ask, confirm, document—not DIY

## Action Steps (Do These Before the Pour)

1. Review the foundation and structural plans in detail.
   - Highlight rebar layouts, footing depths, and any special details.
2. Walk the site and visualize footing and plumbing locations.
   - Picture where bathrooms, kitchens, and main drains will be relative to the slab.
3. Confirm inspection timing with your GC.
   - Ask: "Which inspections need to happen before we pour, and when are they scheduled?"
4. Take photos of rebar, vapor barrier, and rough-ins.
   - Save them in a dedicated "Foundation" folder.
6. Ask your GC to explain the curing plan.
   - Make sure they have a strategy that fits expected weather conditions.

## Scripts & Questions

Use these to keep communication clear and protect the foundation phase.

### *Script: Before Rebar Inspection*

"Before the rebar inspection, can we walk through the foundation plans together so I understand what the inspector will be checking and where the most critical areas are?"

### *Script: Before the Concrete Pour*

"Have all required inspections been completed and approved, and is there anything that needs adjustment or a second look before we actually pour?"

### *Questions to Ask Your GC*

- "Does the rebar layout match the engineering drawings exactly, or were any changes made?"
- "Where will plumbing lines and drains pass through the slab?"
- "How will curing be managed over the first few days?"
- "What weather or temperature conditions would cause us to delay the pour?"

### *Self-Check Questions*

As you approach the pour, ask yourself:

- "Does what I see on site match what's drawn on the plans?"

- "Has anything felt rushed, skipped, or done out of order?"
- "Would fixing a mistake now be easier than after concrete is poured?"

If you're hesitating, that's your cue to pause and get clarity.

## What Comes Next

Once the foundation passes inspection and the concrete has cured, your ADU is ready for framing—the moment when structure turns into shape. Accuracy continues to matter just as much, but now you'll be watching walls, roofs, and shear walls rise from the foundation you just protected.

CHAPTER 7

# FRAMING YOUR ADU CORRECTLY (BEGINNER-FRIENDLY GUIDE)

On two different ADU projects, framing day looked almost identical from the sidewalk—lumber everywhere, nail guns firing, walls rising fast.

- On **Project A,** the crew rushed and "made it work." Walls were slightly out of plumb, headers weren't installed exactly as engineered, and shear wall nailing was sloppy. The framing inspection failed twice. Months later, drywall cracks and sticky doors became permanent reminders of small mistakes.
- On **Project B**, the framing crew worked just as fast, but followed the plans exactly. Walls were straight, connectors were correct, shear walls were nailed like a textbook example. Inspections passed on the first try, trades moved quickly, and the finished ADU felt solid and quiet.

Same city, similar plans. The difference was framing quality.

In every ADU project I've reviewed, framing quality—not finishes—has been the clearest predictor of long-term performance and inspection success.

This chapter is a beginner-friendly guide to framing from an owner-builder's perspective. You won't learn how to swing a hammer—you'll learn what's happening, why it matters, and what you should be looking for while pros do the work.

## Why This Phase Matters

Framing is the moment your ADU stops being an abstract project and becomes a real building. Walls go up. Rooms take shape. The roof defines the form. It's exciting—but it's also one of the highest-risk phases of construction.

Framing creates the structural skeleton of your ADU. Every system that follows—plumbing, electrical, insulation, drywall, cabinetry—depends on the framing being:

- Straight
- Strong
- Precisely built to plan

When framing is done well:

- Inspections pass smoothly
- Trades work faster and cheaper

Doors and windows operate correctly

- Cracks and movement are minimized
- The building performs better during earthquakes

When framing is done poorly, problems compound quickly—and become expensive (or impossible) to fix once the building is closed up.

In the Design-Driven DIY model, framing is one of the Big 3 phases you never DIY yourself. But understanding it will make you far better at:

- Catching obvious issues early
- Asking the right questions
- Documenting work before it's covered

## The Framing Sequence: What Happens and Why It Matters

Good owner-builders don't memorize framing details—they understand the sequence.

You don't need to know every type of stud or connector. What you do need is a basic sense of the order of operations so you can recognize whether work is progressing correctly.

Here's the typical sequence.

### *1. Wall Framing (Built Flat, Then Raised)*

Walls are usually assembled flat on the ground, then lifted into place and braced. Each wall section includes:

- Vertical studs
- Top and bottom plates (horizontal boards at the top and bottom)
- Framing for doors and windows (king studs, jack studs, headers)

Once raised and anchored to the foundation, the wall layout becomes visible—this is when room sizes and circulation finally feel real.

### *Why this step matters:*

- If walls aren't framed to the correct dimensions, room sizes, hallways, and clearances will be wrong.
- If walls aren't straight and plumb, everything later—cabinets, tile, trim, doors—will be harder and more expensive to install.

Errors here affect everything downstream, from cabinet alignment to door swing.

## *2. Sheathing (Turning Pieces into a System)*

After walls are up, sheets of plywood or OSB are nailed to the exterior. This is called sheathing.

Sheathing:

- Locks wall sections together
- Provides lateral strength
- Helps resist wind and earthquakes

Certain walls are designated as shear walls in the engineering plans. On these walls, every detail matters:

- Panel size and orientation
- Nail size
- Nail spacing
- Edge nailing vs. field nailing

These are not suggestions; they are engineered requirements.

## *3. Roof Framing (Rafters or Trusses)*

Next, the roof structure is installed using either:

- Rafters, cut and assembled on-site
- Trusses, pre-engineered units delivered to the site

The choice depends on your design and structural engineering.

### *Why this step matters:*

- Roof framing controls how loads travel down through the walls and into the foundation.
- Small deviations—improper bearing, missing connectors, cut truss members—can create long-term structural stress and inspection problems.

### *4. Roof Decking (Sealing the Shape)*

Sheets of plywood or OSB are nailed over the rafters or trusses to form the roof deck.

At this point:

- The structure feels solid
- The ADU's final shape is clear
- The building is nearly "dry-in ready" once underlayment and roofing are added

The roof deck also acts as a structural diaphragm—another part of the system that helps the building resist lateral forces.

### *5. Door & Window Openings (Precision Zones)*

Door and window openings are precision zones in framing. They require special elements, including headers—horizontal beams that carry the weight above openings.

Header size and material are specified by the engineer and

must be installed exactly as shown.

This is not a judgment call:

- Substituting materials ("We had some leftover 2x8s, so we used those")
- Guessing sizes
- Ignoring specified hangers and connectors

...can lead to inspection failures and structural risk.

## Why Framing Feels Fast—but Isn't Forgiving

Framing days can be exhilarating. Walls seem to appear overnight.

But:

- Framing crews move quickly
- Mistakes are easy to miss in the moment
- Corrections later usually require demolition
- Inspectors are strict at this stage

> Speed is normal. Accuracy is non-negotiable.

## How to Oversee Framing (Without Being "That Owner")

The best owner-builders observe patterns—not individual nails.

You are not there to instruct framers or critique their technique. You are there to:

- Confirm that work matches the structural plans
- Watch for obvious misalignments or missing elements
- Ask about deviations before they're buried or covered

Think of yourself as the quality-control manager, not the carpenter.

Here's what to look for.

### *Plumb & Level*

- Walls should be perfectly vertical (plumb)
- Floors, plates, and key surfaces should be horizontal (level)

Problems here cause:

- Crooked or sticky doors
- Uneven floors
- Visible gaps in trim and finishes
- Cabinets and tile that never quite line up

You don't need fancy tools. Even a long level, a straight board, or your own eye can spot walls that are visibly leaning or floors that feel off.

### *Proper Nailing*

Your engineering plans and structural notes specify:

- Nail size (for example, 8d, 10d)
- Nail spacing (e.g., 4" on center at panel edges, 6" in the field)
- Where additional nailing is required (boundary nailing, drag struts, etc.)

This is especially critical for:

- Exterior walls
- Shear walls
- Roof and floor diaphragms

Improper nailing is one of the most common reasons framing inspections fail. You don't have to count every nail, but you can:

- Spot check areas where nails are obviously too close or too far apart
- Ask your GC or framing lead, "Can you show me where the shear walls are and how you've matched the nail spacing on the plans?"

### *Correct Structural Connections*

Framing isn't just wood; it's also metal. The building relies on connectors like:

- Anchor bolts (connecting walls to the foundation)
- Hold-downs (resisting uplift and lateral forces at shear walls)
- Straps, clips, and hangers (connecting framing members to each other)

These connect:

- Walls to the foundation
- Walls to the roof system
- Beams and headers to posts and supporting walls

Every connector should:

- Match what's called out on the plans (type and location)

- Be properly nailed or screwed (correct fasteners, full pattern)

If you see missing or different hardware than shown on the plans, that's your cue to ask questions before the inspector shows up.

## Framing Red Flags

Pay attention if you notice:

- Missing or obviously substituted metal connectors
- Nail spacing on sheathing that clearly doesn't match the plans
- Walls visibly out of plumb or twisted
- "We always do it this way" when you ask about a plan requirement
- Changes made without engineer or designer approval

Any of these, warrant immediate clarification with your GC, framing lead, or engineer.

## Why Framing Accuracy Pays Off Later

Framing isn't just about passing this week's inspection. Good framing:

- Simplifies electrical and plumbing installation (straight, predictable pathways)
- Reduces drywall cracking and nail pops
- Speeds up finish work (less shimming, fewer weird patches)

- Improves energy performance (stud alignment, fewer gaps)
- Protects resale value (solid doors, smooth floors, fewer "mystery" issues)

Poor framing creates problems that surface months or years later—long after the crew has moved on and the warranty has expired.

As the owner-builder, your attention here is one of the best long-term investments you can make.

## Your Role as the Owner-Builder

You are the quality-control manager—not the carpenter.

During framing, your responsibilities are to:

- Reference the structural drawings
- Confirm that what you see matches the plans
- Ask questions early, before work is covered
- Schedule and track inspections with your GC
- Document progress with photos, especially shear walls and connectors

*You don't build. You verify.*

## The Owner-Builder Mindset

If you come from a non-construction background, it's easy to feel like you're "in the way" when you ask questions.

You're not.

- You're the one paying for the work
- You're the one living with the results
- You're the one protecting the structural integrity of your ADU

*You're not slowing the project down. You're protecting it.*

## A Quick Review:Chapter Checklist

Before moving on, confirm:

- I understand the basic framing sequence (walls → sheathing → roof → openings)
- I know the difference between rafters and trusses
- I know what a shear wall is and why it matters
- I know what to look for during framing (plumb, level, nailing, connectors)
- I understand why framing inspections are strictI'm clear that my role is to observe and verify, not to DIY framing

## Action Steps (Do These During Framing)

1. Review the structural framing plans before framing starts.
   - Identify shear walls, key headers, and major connectors.
2. Walk the site daily (or as often as allowed) during active framing.

- Look for obvious plumb/level issues and missing connectors.

3. Take photos of shear walls and connectors before they're covered.
    - Create a "Framing & Shear Walls" folder in your ADU binder or phone.
4. Confirm inspection timing with your GC.
    - Ask: "What needs to be complete and visible for framing inspection?"
5. Ask questions immediately—before the crew moves on.
    - If something looks different from the plans, pause and ask for an explanation.

## Scripts & Questions

Use or adapt these to keep framing aligned with the engineering and your expectations.

### *Script: Before Framing Begins*

*"Before framing starts, can we review the framing and shear wall plans together so I understand what the inspector will be looking for and where the most critical structural elements are?"*

### *Script: During Framing*

*"Before we move past this section, can we confirm that all required connectors, headers, and shear wall nailing match the engineering drawings—and take a few photos for my records?"*

### *Questions to Ask Your GC or Framing Crew*

- "Can you show me where the shear walls are and how they match the plan details?"
- "Are any substitutions being made for connectors, headers, or lumber sizes?"
- "Is everything in place and visible for the framing inspection?"
- "Will anything be covered before inspection, or can we keep critical areas open?

### *Self-Check Questions*

As framing progresses, ask yourself:

- "Does what I see in the field match what's drawn on the plans?"
- "Have I documented key framing elements—shear walls, connectors, major headers?"
- "Would an inspector flag anything obvious (crooked walls, missing hardware, sloppy nailing)?"

If the answer to any of these is "I'm not sure," that's your cue to pause and ask your GC, framing lead, or engineer for clarification.

## What Comes Next

Once framing passes inspection, your ADU transitions from structure to systems: plumbing, electrical, and mechanical rough-ins. Precision still matters—but now it's about pipes, wires, and ducts threading through the skeleton you've just watched take shape.

# PART III

## YOUR DIY ROADMAP

CHAPTER 8

# AFTER THE PROS LEAVE: WHAT YOU CAN SAFELY DIY

On two nearly identical ADU projects, the numbers told a surprising story:

- **Homeowner A** hired pros for everything—from site prep to the final coat of paint. The project turned out beautifully, but the budget stretched painfully, with a big chunk going to simple tasks they could have done themselves.
- **Homeowner B** hired pros for the Big 3, rough trades, and inspections—then took over at finishes. They spent evenings and weekends installing insulation, painting, laying click-together flooring, and hanging doors and trim. The ADU looked just as polished, but their total cost was tens of thousands lower.

> Same structure. Same safety. Very different labor bill.

In nearly every successful Design-Driven DIY ADU, the biggest savings happen after the structural work is complete—not before.

This chapter is about that phase—what you can safely DIY

once the pros have finished the risky stuff.

## Why This Phase Matters

Once the structural shell is complete and rough inspections are approved, the most intimidating part of your ADU build is officially behind you:

- Your foundation is solid
- The framing is straight
- The building is dried in (roofed and weather-protected)
- Rough plumbing, electrical, and mechanical have passed inspection

This is the turning point.

From here on, the work becomes:

- Slower and more detailed
- Far less risky
- Easier to learn
- Flexible around evenings and weekends

This is where homeowners gain the most control, confidence, and financial payoff—without compromising safety or code compliance.

## Understanding the DIY Phase: Think in Layers, Not Tasks

DIY success isn't about skill—it's about sequence.

The finish phase works best when you think in layers. Each step prepares the next. Skipping ahead or working out of order almost always creates rework later.

> Your goal is not raw speed. Your goal is clean progression.

### *The #1 DIY Mistake*

Starting the "fun stuff" too early.

- Cabinets installed before walls are fully prepped
- Flooring laid before painting is finished
- Trim installed before final sanding or touch-ups

These often get **damaged, removed, or redone.** The sequence protects your effort—and your budget.

## The Recommended DIY Sequence (Step-by-Step)

Homeowners who follow a clear finish sequence spend less time fixing mistakes—and more time actually finishing.

Assuming your shell, roof, and rough trades are complete and inspected, here's a beginner-friendly order that works well for most Design-Driven DIY builds.

### *1. Exterior Finishes (Seal the Building First)*

Before you move inside, complete exterior work:

- Siding

- Exterior trim
- Exterior paint or stain

Why this comes first:

- Protects the structure from moisture
- Reduces stress during interior work (less worry about weather)
- Prevents damage to interior finishes from exterior ladders, tools, and debris

Many modern siding systems are repetitive and very DIY-friendly—especially if you're comfortable on ladders and able to work safely.

### 2. Insulation (Beginner-Friendly, High Impact)

Next, install insulation in walls and ceilings using materials like:

- Fiberglass batts
- Mineral wool (rock wool)
- In some cases, rigid foam (where specified)

Benefits:

- Improves comfort and sound control
- Boosts energy efficiency
- Easy to learn with clear manufacturer instructions
- Low risk—mistakes are usually easy to spot and correct

This is one of the best confidence-building DIY steps and a great way to get comfortable working inside your ADU.

### 3. Drywall (Where the Space Becomes Real)

Drywall is where your ADU starts looking like a real interior:

- Hanging sheets
- Taping seams
- Applying joint compound
- Sanding smooth

This step is:

- Physically demanding
- Dusty
- Very achievable if you:
    - Work one room at a time
    - Accept "good enough" over "perfect"
    - Go slowly and allow proper drying time between coats

Many homeowners DIY drywall successfully—others choose to hang it themselves and hire a pro to tape/finish. Both are valid approaches.

### 4. Interior Paint (Maximum Impact, Minimum Risk)

After drywall is finished and sanded, it's time to prime and paint.

Why this is a top DIY task:

- Immediate visual transformation
- Huge labor savings
- Forgiving learning curve
- You have total control over color and quality

Painting is one of the highest return-on-effort DIY tasks in an ADU. Good prep (tape, drop cloths, sanding) matters more than fancy techniques.

### *5. Flooring (Save Big, Work at Your Pace)*

Once walls and ceilings are painted, install flooring. DIY-friendly options include:

- Laminate
- Luxury vinyl plank (LVP)
- Some engineered wood products

Most modern systems:

- Use locking mechanisms that click together
- Require no glue and minimal fasteners
- Allow you to work room-by-room, at your own pace

Install flooring after painting to avoid splatters and damage.

### *6. Interior Doors & Trim (Polish Phase Begins)*

Now you start adding the details that make the space feel finished:

- Interior doors and frames
- Baseboards
- Window and door casings
- Simple moldings (if included in your design)

This step:

- Dramatically elevates how "finished" the ADU feels
- Rewards careful measuring and cutting

- Benefits from patience more than strength

Even basic trim work can transform the space—and it's all firmly in the DIY sweet spot for many homeowners.

## 7. Cabinets & Countertops (Function Arrives)

Next, install:

- Kitchen cabinets
- Bathroom vanities
- Countertops (pre-fabricated or simple tops; complex stone may be pro-installed)

Key tips:

- Take extra time to level and plumb every cabinet
- Use shims and a long level
- Follow manufacturer instructions precisely

This is often the moment the ADU finally feels "real" as a place where people will live.

## 8. Tile Work (Precision Over Speed)

Common DIY tile areas include:

- Bathroom floors
- Kitchen backsplashes
- Small accent areas

Many homeowners:

- DIY floor and backsplash tile
- Hire out shower waterproofing and shower walls for peace of mind

Tile rewards patience and careful layout—not speed. Take time to:

- Plan layout and cut lines
- Use the right trowel and mortar
- Allow proper cure times

### *9. Plumbing & Electrical Fixtures*

At this stage, the rough plumbing and electrical are already done and inspected by licensed trades.

Your DIY focus is on visible fixtures only, such as:

- Toilets (setting on wax rings, bolting down)
- Sinks and faucets (connecting to existing supply and drain stubs)
- Light fixtures (swapping from temp lights to final fixtures)
- Switch and outlet cover plates

Local codes vary, so always confirm what's allowed for homeowners. The key principle:

***Rough systems = pros.***

***Fixtures and finishes = often DIY-safe.***

### *10. Final Touches (Completion Details)*

Finally, you add the small details that tie everything together:

- Mirrors
- Towel bars and hooks
- Closet rods and shelving

- Door hardware
- Window coverings
- Paint touch-ups and caulk lines

These finishing touches:

- Take surprisingly little time
- Have a big impact on how polished the ADU feels
- Are easy to tweak or adjust later

## Why This Phase Is Ideal for DIY

This phase is where DIY and Design-Driven work perfectly together.

These tasks:

- Don't affect structural safety
- Allow mistakes to be corrected relatively easily
- Fit around real-life schedules (evenings and weekends)
- Offer maximum labor savings for the risk involved
- Reward care and patience more than years of experience

> This is where patience beats expertise.

## Your Role as the Owner-Builder (Now It Changes)

Up to this point, your role has been:

- Coordinating pros
- Verifying structure and systems
- Managing inspections and contracts

At this stage, your role shifts:

> You stop supervising and start crafting.

Your responsibilities now include:

- Following a reasonable sequence (inside and out)
- Reading and following manufacturer instructions
- Scheduling any remaining inspections (finals, smoke/CO alarms, etc.)
- Pacing yourself realistically to avoid burnout
- Protecting finished work as you move through tasks

This phase is about quality control and consistency, not bragging rights for doing everything fast.

## A Better Definition of "DIY"

> DIY does not mean "do everything yourself." It means doing the right things yourself.

You're still allowed to hire help for any step that feels overwhelming, dangerous, or beyond your bandwidth. The goal is a safe, high-quality ADU—not a personal suffering contest.

## A Quick Review: Chapter Checklist

Before moving on, confirm:

- ☐ I understand the recommended DIY finish sequence (outside → insulation → drywall → paint → floors → trim → cabinets → tile → fixtures → final touches)
- ☐ I know which tasks are safest and most sensible to DIY
- ☐ I understand that exterior work should be completed early to protect the shell
- ☐ I see why order matters and how it prevents damage and rework
- ☐ I know which tasks may still require inspections or pro involvement
- ☐ I feel confident pacing myself instead of rushing to the finish line

## Action Steps (Do These Before You Start DIY Work)

1. Print or write your DIY sequence checklist.
   - Post it in your ADU or project binder.
2. Decide which tasks you'll DIY and which you'll outsource.
   - Be honest about your time, energy, and interest.

3. Gather basic tools for early tasks:
   - Insulation tools (utility knife, stapler, safety gear)
   - Painting supplies (rollers, brushes, trays, tape, drop cloths)
   - Flooring tools (tapping block, spacers, saw suitable for cuts)
4. Watch 1–2 high-quality tutorials per task before starting.
   - Focus on tools, safety, and common mistakes.
5. Create a realistic evening/weekend schedule.
   - Break tasks into small, achievable chunks (e.g., "insulate one room," "prime walls," "floor the bedroom").

## Scripts & Questions

### *Script: Transitioning from Pros to DIY*

*"Now that rough inspections are approved, can you confirm which work is fully complete, which inspections remain, and whether there's anything that must be done by licensed trades before I begin finish work?"*

### *Questions to Ask Yourself Before Each DIY Task*

- "Does this task affect structure or safety?"
- "Has the previous step been fully completed and inspected if required?"
- "Would doing this later be easier—or am I jumping ahead?"
- "Can I undo or redo this if I make a mistake?"

If your answers make you uneasy, pause and reconsider—maybe this one belongs to a pro.

### *Script: Scheduling Final Inspections*

*"I've completed the homeowner-installed finish work. Can you confirm which final inspections are required before occupancy and what needs to be ready for each?"*

### *Self-Check Questions*

As you move through the finish phase, keep asking:

- "Am I following the sequence—or skipping ahead because I'm excited?"
- "Am I rushing because I'm tired, or trying to 'just get it done'?"
- "Would slowing down and doing one more round of prep improve the result?"

If the honest answer is "yes," give yourself permission to slow down. Finish work is where care really shows.

## What Comes Next

Once finishes are complete and all final inspections are approved, your project reaches its last big milestone: the Certificate of Occupancy the official moment your ADU becomes a legal, livable space.

CHAPTER 9

# INSULATION, DRYWALL & INTERIOR WALLS

On most DIY-managed ADU projects, this is where something shifts.

- At first, homeowners are nervous about every detail—permits, inspections, engineering, foundations.
- Then they hit insulation and drywall, and suddenly the work feels learnable, repeatable, and the visual progress is huge.

You'll hang a few sheets, mud a few seams, and realize:

> "Oh. I'm actually doing this."

In most DIY-managed ADUs, this is the phase where homeowners gain real momentum—because the work is learnable, repeatable, and the results show fast.

This chapter shows you how to handle insulation and drywall in a way that's beginner-friendly, code-aware, and realistic.

## Why This Phase Matters (Read First)

Once your structural shell is complete and rough inspections have passed, you're no longer building a structure—you're building a living space.

Insulation and drywall determine how your ADU feels day-to-day:

- Comfort (temperature control)
- Quiet (sound reduction between rooms and from outside)
- Finish quality (how "professional" the interior looks)
- Energy compliance (meeting code requirements and energy reports)

This phase is ideal for the Design-Driven DIY model because it's:

- Low structural risk
- Highly teachable
- Made of clear, repeatable stepsFull of "fixable" mistakes

Your job is to respect the sequence, take your time, and protect the work you've already paid pros to complete.

## The Winning Mindset for This Chapter

Drywall and insulation aren't about talent.

They're about sequence, patience, and consistency.

You don't need to be an artist. You just need to:

- Follow the right order
- Use the right tools
- Accept steady progress over Instagram perfection

## Tools & Materials (Get Ready Before You Start)

The fastest way to ruin drywall work is to start without the right tools—then rush to "make it work."

Gather supplies before you begin so you're not stopping mid-wall, mid-coat, or mid-sanding.

### *Basic Tools*

- Utility knife
- Tape measure
- Straight edge / drywall square
- Drill or drywall screw gun
- Drywall saw or rotary cutting tool
- Putty knives (6", 10", 12")
- Mud pan
- Sanding block or pole sander
- Step ladder
- (Optional but very helpful) Shop vacuum + dust control setup
- Safety gear: dust mask or respirator, safety glasses, gloves, hearing protection

### *Materials*

- Insulation batts (fiberglass or mineral wool, as specified by your plans)

- Drywall sheets (commonly ½" for walls, ⅝" for ceilings—follow your plans and local code)
- Drywall screws
- Joint tape (paper or mesh; many pros prefer paper with a good mud)
- Joint compound ("mud") — all-purpose or separate taping/topcoats
- Corner bead (for outside corners)
- Caulk and foam for sealing small gaps (where appropriate)

Staging everything in one place before you start will make the work feel calmer and more controlled.

## Step 1 – Insulation (Warmth, Comfort, Quiet)

Insulation is one of the highest-impact DIY tasks because it improves comfort immediately—and it's hard to mess up if you follow the basics.

What Insulation Does

- Keeps the ADU cooler in summer and warmer in winter
- Reduces outside noise and sound between rooms
- Improves energy efficiency and helps meet energy code
- Supports the performance assumptions in your energy (Title 24) report

Installing Insulation: Simple Rules That Work

- Batts should fit snugly—not bulging or loose
- Cut cleanly around electrical boxes and obstructions

- Don't pack insulation tightly into cavities (compressed insulation = reduced R-value)
- Fill small cavities (above doors, around windows) with properly cut pieces
- Work one wall or one bay at a time so you don't miss sections

If you're using mineral wool, be extra careful with protective gear—it sheds more fibers. Always check your energy report or local code for specific R-values required.

### Common Insulation Mistakes

Watch out for:

- Compressing batts (reduces performance and R-value)
- Leaving gaps at corners, edges, or behind wires and boxes
- Forgetting small cavities (above doors, narrow strips, around windows)
- Skipping protective gear (itchy arms now, regret later)

Slow down, fit pieces carefully, and take a quick photo of each wall when you're done—it's nice documentation for you and inspectors.

## Step 2 – Hanging Drywall (Turning a Shell into Rooms)

Once drywall is up, the ADU stops feeling like a jobsite and starts feeling like a home.

Drywall is physically demanding but not technically complex. It's like hanging large, heavy sheets of paper on a grid.

### Drywall Basics

- Sheets are screwed to framing (studs, ceiling joists)
- Seams between sheets are normal and will be taped and mudded later
- Screw placement matters for strength and clean finishing

### Key Tips That Prevent Problems

- Measure carefully before cutting—cut once, adjust as needed
- Stagger seams (don't line up vertical joints on adjacent rows)
- Use proper screw spacing (commonly 12" on ceilings, 16" on walls—check code/plan notes)
- Drive screws just below the surface, creating a small dimple—don't tear the paper
- Use a helper or drywall lift whenever possible (your back will thank you)
- Hang ceilings first, then walls

If something doesn't fit perfectly, don't panic. Small gaps can be filled with mud; huge gaps signal you should recut.

### Quick "Good Drywall" Checklist

As you hang, spot-check:

- ☐ Seams are staggered, not stacked in a straight line
- ☐ Screws are slightly dimpled, not ripped through paper

- ☐ Cutouts (outlets, switches, can lights) are clean and reasonably tight
- ☐ No major gaps at joints that would require mountains of mud

Perfection isn't required. You're aiming for sound structure and reasonable alignment.

## Step 3 – Taping & Mudding (The Real Skill Is Patience)

DIY drywall finishing looks hard because people try to do it fast. Slow work is good work here.

What It Means

- Tape covers seams between sheets
- Joint compound (mud) covers tape and screw holes
- Multiple thin coats create smooth walls and soft edges

The Simplified Process

1. Apply tape over seams (embedded in a thin layer of mud, if using paper tape).
2. Apply a thin coat of compound over the tape and screw heads.
3. Let it dry fully—don't rush this; rushing equals failure.
4. Sand lightly to knock down ridges and bumps.
5. Apply a second, slightly wider coat.
6. Let dry, sand lightly.
7. Apply a third, wider feather coat if needed for smoothness.

Always remember:

Thin coats beat thick coats—every time. Thick coats crack,

shrink, and create more sanding work later.

*"Good Enough" Is the Goal*

Most walls don't need to be gallery-perfect.

They need to:

- Look smooth under normal lighting
- Disappear once primed and painted
- Feel largely flat to the touch

If a tiny imperfection is only visible when you shine a flashlight at a sharp angle, you're probably fine.

## Step 4 – Smooth, Paint-Ready Walls

After final sanding, something magical happens: your ADU stops looking like a construction project and starts feeling like a bright, continuous interior.

Pro Tips for Better Results

- Thin coats, every time, even if it feels slower
- Let layers dry fully—don't "help" them with heaters or fans that dry too fast
- Sand with side-lighting (a work light along the wall) to reveal ridges and dips
- Don't over-sand; you're smoothing, not grinding back to the paper
- Accept steady progress: one room at a time, not the whole ADU at once

Once you're happy with the surface, you're ready to move into priming and painting (covered in more detail in the finishes chapter).

## Why This Phase Is Ideal for DIY

This is the chapter where most homeowners shift from "Can I do this?" to "I'm doing this."

Insulation and drywall:

- Don't affect structural safety when framing and rough trades are already inspected
- Have clear, repeatable steps
- Allow corrections and second attempts
- Create fast visual progress
- Build confidence for later phases like flooring, trim, and cabinets

You'll see tangible improvement every day you work—which is incredibly motivating.

### *Your Role as the Owner-Builder*

Your job here is not speed. It's control.

- Work methodically, one wall or room at a time
- Follow the sequence (insulation → hang → tape → mud → sand)
- Stop when tired—fatigue causes crooked cuts and sloppy mud
- Protect finished surfaces as you go (cover floors, tape edges)
- Keep momentum through small, consistent wins, not marathon sessions

By the end of this phase, your ADU will feel like a real interior—not a construction site—and you'll be much more confident in your own capabilities.

## Chapter Checklist (Quick Review)

Before moving on, confirm:

- ☐ I have the right tools and materials staged and ready
- ☐ I understand insulation basics (snug fit, no compression, no gaps)
- ☐ I know drywall hanging priorities (seams, screws, clean cutouts, ceilings first)
- ☐ I understand the mudding process (thin coats, dry time, light sanding in between)
- ☐ I know what "paint-ready" walls actually look like under normal lighting
- ☐ I'm prepared to pace this work realistically—one room at a time

## Action Steps (Do These Today or This Weekend)

1. **Buy or borrow all drywall tools before you start.**
   - Don't rely on improvising once the first sheet is up.
2. **Pick one wall and complete insulation end-to-end.**
   - Use it as a test run and confidence booster.
3. **Watch one full drywall finishing tutorial (from tape → mud → sand).**
   - Look for someone working in realistic conditions, not

a sped-up highlight reel.

4. **Create a realistic schedule: one room at a time.**
   - For example: "This weekend: insulate and hang drywall in the bedroom."
5. **Set up dust control early.**
   - Plastic barriers, a shop vac, and good masks will save your sanity.

## Scripts & Questions You Can Use

### *Script: Confirming You're Ready to Start*

*"Rough inspections are approved—can you confirm there are no remaining in-wall changes or penetrations needed before I insulate and close up the walls?"*

### *Questions to Ask Yourself Before Hanging Drywall*

- "Are all in-wall systems (plumbing, electrical, HVAC, low-voltage) completed and inspected?"
- "Do I know where shutoffs, cleanouts, and any access points are?"
- "Have I photographed wall cavities for future reference—especially around plumbing and wiring?"

If the answer to any of these is "no," pause and address it before covering walls.

### *Script: Getting Drywall Help (If Needed)*

*"I'm planning to DIY most of the drywall, but I'd like professional help with either hanging ceilings or final finishing. Can you quote those as separate line items so I can decide where to bring you in?"*

### *Questions to Ask a Paint/Finish Supplier*

- "What primer works best for freshly finished drywall in a new build?"
- "What sheen do you recommend for small spaces like ADUs—especially for walls vs. trim?"
- "What's the most forgiving paint if my walls have minor imperfections?"

CHAPTER 10

# DIY FLOORING, TRIM & DOORS

In DIY-managed ADU builds, there's one phase where homeowners experience the biggest leap from construction site to finished home—with the least risk.

Across DIY-managed ADUs, flooring, trim, and doors deliver the most dramatic "finished-home" transformation because this is detail work, not structural work.

By this stage, the heavy lifting is behind you. The structure is complete, the walls are finished, and paint is on the walls. Now, flooring, trim, and interior doors bring everything together—visually, functionally, and emotionally.

This chapter focuses on some of the **best DIY opportunities in the entire build**, because these tasks are:

- Low risk to structural safety
- Learnable with basic tools
- Repeatable, one room at a time
- Highly visible, with fast payoff
- Forgiving—most mistakes are fixable

Done carefully, this phase improves not just how your ADU looks, but how it feels to live in: comfort underfoot, reduced noise, clean transitions, and long-term durability.

> You're not trying to work fast. You're trying to work clean.

Accuracy, sequencing, and consistency matter more than speed here. This is where patience shows.

Choosing the Right Flooring for Your ADU

The best flooring choice is the one you can install correctly—and live with happily for years.

Flooring affects how your ADU looks, feels, and holds up over time. For most ADUs—especially rentals or high-use spaces—the ideal flooring should be:

- Water-resistant
- Scratch-resistant
- Comfortable underfoot
- Easy to clean
- DIY-friendly to install and repair

There are many flooring options, but one consistently checks the most boxes for owner-builders.

## Why Luxury Vinyl Plank (LVP) Is a Popular Choice

Luxury Vinyl Plank (LVP) has become a favorite among ADU builders because it balances appearance, performance, and DIY simplicity.

LVP typically:

- Mimics real wood convincingly
- Handles moisture well (ideal for kitchens and bath-

rooms)

- Uses click-lock systems designed for DIY installation
- Allows damaged planks to be replaced without redoing the entire floor

For many homeowners, it's the best single-floor solution if you want a consistent look throughout the ADU without complicated transitions.

### *When LVP Is Especially Smart*

LVP shines in:

- ◊ Rental units
- ◊ Homes with kids or pets
- ◊ ADUs with kitchens and bathrooms sharing the same flooring
- ◊ DIY timelines spread over evenings and weekends

It's not the only good option—but it's often the most forgiving.

### *Installing LVP Flooring*

Most flooring failures come from prep—not installation.

LVP installation is systematic and forgiving if you set yourself up properly.

## The Basic Installation Process

### *1. Prepare the subfloor*

The subfloor must be clean, dry, and flat. Scrape high spots and fill low areas before you begin. Small imperfections telegraph through finished flooring.

### *2. Install underlayment (if required)*

Some LVP products include built-in padding; others require a separate underlayment. Always follow the manufacturer's instructions.

### *3. Plan your layout*

Starting straight and square is what makes the finished floor look professional. A little planning here prevents awkward slivers at the far wall.

### *4. Install planks row by row*

Click-lock edges connect with gentle pressure and tapping. Never force joints—misalignment is the problem, not the plank.

### *5. Cut planks for edges and doorways*

A utility knife, jigsaw, or small saw is usually enough. Take your time around doorways and transitions.

Key point: This is slow work. Slow is fine.

Accuracy is what makes it look expensive.

## Flooring Mistakes to Avoid

- ◊ Skipping subfloor flattening
- ◊ Forgetting expansion gaps at walls
- ◊ Starting out of square

- ◊ Forcing joints instead of correcting alignment
- ◊ Installing flooring without planning trim and door transitions

Flooring usually goes after paint but before baseboards and door casings, so trim can cover expansion gaps cleanly.

## Trim Work: Baseboards & Casings (The "Polish" Layer)

Trim doesn't just decorate—it makes the entire space look intentional.

Trim frames the edges of your work and covers inevitable gaps. This typically includes:

- Baseboards along the floor
- Door casings around frames
- Window trim (if your design includes it)

> Good trim is subtle. Bad trim is obvious.

### *Why Trim Work Is Ideal for DIY*

Trim is especially DIY-friendly because:

- Materials are affordable
- Mistakes are replaceable
- The visual improvement is immediate
- Repetition builds skill quickly

You'll get better with each room—and the learning curve is forgiving.

### *Basic Trim Installation Steps*

1. Measure carefully and cut precisely
2. Dry-fit pieces before fastening
3. Secure trim with finish nails into framing
4. Fill nail holes and caulk seams for a clean finish

> Trim rewards patience, not strength.

## The "Gap Rule"

Small gaps = caulk.

Big gaps = recut and re-fit.

Don't caulk your way out of bad measurements.

Hanging Interior Doors (Pre-Hung = Beginner-Friendly)

If you can level and shim carefully, you can install pre-hung doors.

Interior doors add privacy, sound control, and that final "home" feeling. Most DIY builders use pre-hung doors, which arrive already mounted in a frame.

### *Why Pre-Hung Doors Are Easier*

With pre-hung doors:

- Hinges are already installed
- Alignment is mostly done at the factory
- Your job is to place and secure the frame correctly

This turns a complex carpentry task into a manageable, repeatable process.

### Basic Door Installation Process

1. Place the door and frame into the rough opening
2. Shim until the frame is plumb and level
3. Secure the frame to the wall framing
4. Test swing and latch alignment
5. Install casing to hide gaps

Your first door will take the longest. Each one after that goes faster.

### Door Success Test

A properly installed door:

- Swings smoothly
- Stays open or closed without drifting
- Latches without force

If any of these fail, adjust the shims before installing trim.

## Why Flooring, Trim & Doors Are Perfect DIY Projects

These tasks:

- Don't affect structural safety
- Allow corrections without major demolition
- Can be completed one room at a time
- Produce fast, visible progress

- Build confidence for the final stretch

This is often the moment homeowners shift from:

"I hope this works" to "I've got this."

## Your Role as the Owner-Builder

At this stage, quality comes from consistency—doing simple steps carefully every time.

Your focus should be:

- Methodical progress
- Following manufacturer instructions
- Accuracy over speed
- Protecting finished work as you move forward
- Taking pride in the details

Every plank, casing, and door isn't just progress—it's proof that smart planning is paying off.

## A Quick Review: Chapter Checklist

Before moving on, confirm:

- ☐ I've chosen a DIY-friendly flooring material
- ☐ I understand subfloor prep and layout planning
- ☐ I know the basic LVP installation sequence
- ☐ I understand trim components and installation steps
- ☐ I know how pre-hung doors are shimmed and secured
- ☐ I'm working room-by-room with realistic pacing

## Action Steps

- Order flooring with 10–15% extra for waste and mistakes
- Stage tools: spacers, tapping block, miter saw, shims, nailer or hammer
- Practice trim cuts in a less-visible area first
- Install one door completely before moving to the next
- Keep a running punch list instead of stopping momentum for small fixes

## Scripts & Questions You Can Use

### Before Flooring Starts

*"Is all messy work—especially drywall sanding and painting—complete before I install flooring?"*

### At the Flooring Store

- "Does this product require underlayment?"
- "What expansion gap do you recommend?"
- "Can individual planks be replaced later?"

### When Something Doesn't Fit

*"I'm going to stop and re-measure before I cut again. One accurate cut saves two repairs."*

## *Self-Check Questions*

- "Am I rushing because I'm tired?"
- "Does this room look cleaner and more precise than the last one?"
- "Did I protect finished surfaces as I moved forward?"

CHAPTER 11

# KITCHENS & BATHROOMS: SAVING WITHOUT SACRIFICING QUALITY

In nearly every ADU I've reviewed, kitchens and bathrooms go over budget for the same reason:

> Not because of materials—but because of labor decisions made too early.

These rooms are the most expensive spaces in any ADU, and also the most visible. Cabinets, countertops, fixtures, tile, and appliances add up quickly. When everything is fully hired out, labor alone can double the final cost.

The good news is this:

> Kitchens and bathrooms also offer the biggest opportunity for smart, controlled savings.

With the right materials and a selective DIY approach, you can build kitchens and bathrooms that feel durable, modern, and high-end—without paying custom pricing or contractor mark-ups.

## The Core Strategy

> Spend on what you touch every day. Save on what's repeatable and installable.

This chapter shows you where quality truly matters—and where careful DIY can deliver professional results at a fraction of the cost.

### *Understanding Where the Money Really Goes*

In kitchens and baths, labor often costs more than the materials themselves.

The biggest cost drivers are usually:

- Cabinet installation
- Countertop installation
- Tile labor
- Fixture installation

Many of these tasks are priced high because they're time-consuming, not because they're technically complex. By choosing materials designed for homeowner installation—and by sequencing the work carefully—you can eliminate a large portion of these labor costs without cutting corners.

## Ready-to-Assemble (RTA) Cabinets: Big Savings, Clean Look

High-quality RTA cabinets now rival custom cabinets in appearance—at a fraction of the cost.

Cabinets are often the single largest expense in a kitchen. Custom cabinets look great—but they come with custom pricing, long lead times, and limited flexibility. For ADUs, RTA cabinets are often the smarter choice.

### Why RTA Cabinets Work So Well in ADUs

RTA cabinets:

- Ship flat and assemble on site
- Cost significantly less than custom cabinetry
- Include modern features like soft-close hinges and drawers
- Are designed specifically for DIY installation

When assembled and installed carefully, they are nearly indistinguishable from custom cabinets—especially once countertops, hardware, and backsplashes are in place.

### Basic RTA Cabinet Installation (Simplified)

1. Assemble cabinet boxes according to manufacturer instructions
2. Locate and mark wall studs
3. Install upper cabinets first
4. Install base cabinets, shimming and leveling carefully
5. Secure cabinets to each other for a seamless run

> Key principle: Leveling matters more than speed.

Take your time here. Cabinets set the reference for countertops, tile, and appliances.

Cabinet Installation Red Flags

- Rushing leveling
- Skipping stud attachment
- Installing base cabinets before uppers
- Ignoring manufacturer spacing requirements

If cabinets aren't level and secure, every downstream task becomes harder.

## DIY-Friendly Countertops: Why Butcher Block Works

For ADUs, butcher block often delivers the best balance of cost, warmth, and DIY control.

Stone and quartz countertops can blow a budget fast—especially once fabrication, templating, and professional installation are added. Butcher block offers a practical, attractive alternative that works well with DIY timelines.

Why Butcher Block Is a Smart ADU Choice

- Lower cost than stone or quartz
- Cuttable with standard tools
- Warm, inviting appearance
- Repairable and refinishable
- Flexible for staged DIY installation

Basic Installation Steps

1. Dry-fit countertop pieces
2. Cut sink openings if needed

3. Secure countertop to cabinets
4. Sand edges and surface
5. Seal thoroughly—especially near sinks

Important: Sealing protects against moisture and staining.

Don't rush this step.

## Countertop Reality Check

Butcher block looks best when maintained.

It's a lifestyle choice—not a "set it and forget it" surface.

For many ADUs, that trade-off is well worth the savings and visual warmth.

Tile Backsplashes: High Impact, Low Risk

A backsplash is one of the most satisfying DIY upgrades because the area is small and the payoff is huge.

Why Backsplashes Are DIY-Friendly

- Limited square footage
- Affordable materials
- Mistakes are fixable early
- Major visual impact

Basic Backsplash Installation Process

1. Prep wall surface
2. Plan tile layout carefully
3. Apply tile adhesive
4. Set tiles using spacers
5. Grout and clean

Simple patterns—like subway tile or straight-stack layouts—reduce complexity and age better over time.

Simple patterns install cleaner, faster, and more predictably—especially for first-time DIYers.

## Bathroom Fixtures: Vanities & Toilets

Once rough plumbing is inspected, fixture installation becomes a finish task—not a technical one.

### *Installing a Bathroom Vanity*

- Position vanity against wall
- Secure to wall studs
- Install sink and faucet
- Connect plumbing

Vanities allow adjustment time, which makes them ideal for careful DIYers.

### *Installing a Toilet*

- Install wax ring
- Set toilet carefully and evenly
- Secure without overtighteningConnect water supply

This is a common DIY task with clear instructions and minimal tools.

There's no penalty for calling a pro when something feels off.

## Where to Spend vs. Where to Save

### *Spend On*

- Cabinet hardware
- Faucets and fixtures
- Lighting
- Proper waterproofing

### *Save On*

- Cabinet installation labor
- Simple countertops
- Straightforward tile layouts
- Fixture installation labor

Smart spending choices make the space feel premium without overspending.

## Why Kitchens & Bathrooms Are Ideal for Strategic DIY

These tasks:

- Don't affect structural safety
- Follow documented installation steps
- Allow corrections and adjustments
- Deliver high visual impact
- Give you full control over quality

This is where planning beats budget.

## Your Role as the Owner-Builder

At this stage, craftsmanship shows in the details—not the price tag.

Focus on:

- Careful measuring and leveling
- Following manufacturer instructions
- Accuracy over speed
- Clean finishes
- Pride in the details

When done thoughtfully, your kitchen and bathroom will feel professional, durable, and inviting—without the cost of a fully custom build.

## A Quick Review: Chapter Checklist

Before moving on, confirm:

- ☐ I understand where kitchen and bath costs really come from
- ☐ I know which tasks are safe and sensible to DIY
- ☐ I understand RTA cabinet installation basics
- ☐ I know why butcher block works well for ADUs
- ☐ I know where to spend and where to save
- ☐ I'm prioritizing accuracy over speed

## Action Steps

1. Finalize cabinet layout and measurements
2. Order cabinets and countertops with a time buffer
3. Watch one full cabinet installation walkthrough
4. Dry-fit tile layouts before applying adhesive
5. Keep a punch list instead of fixing everything immediately

## Scripts & Questions You Can Use

### *Before Installing Cabinets*

*"Are walls finished, floors installed, and measurements double-checked before I anchor anything?"*

### *Questions to Ask the Cabinet Supplier*

- "Are these cabinets square once assembled?"
- "What wall clearance is required?"
- "Are filler or trim pieces needed for a clean finish?"

### *Before Connecting Plumbing Fixtures*

*"Has all rough plumbing passed inspection, and are shutoffs accessible?"*

### *Self-Check Questions*

- "Am I rushing because I want this done?"

- "Would slowing down improve alignment or finish quality?"
- "Does this installation look clean and intentional?"

If the answer to any of these is "no," pause. The details here are what people notice most.

## What Comes Next

With kitchens and bathrooms complete, your ADU enters its final stretch: punch lists, final inspections, and the last milestone—the Certificate of Occupancy, when your ADU officially becomes a legal, livable home

CHAPTER 12

# PAINTING, FIXTURES & FINAL TOUCHES

In nearly every ADU project I've seen, the difference between finished and impressive isn't structural.

It's the final 5%—painting, fixtures, and details.

This chapter covers that last stretch: the work that transforms your ADU from a construction project into a space that feels intentional, comfortable, and complete.

## Why This Phase Matters

You've reached the final stretch. The structure is complete, major installations are done, and now the focus shifts to the details that shape how the space is experienced.

Painting, fixtures, and final touches may seem minor compared to framing or foundations—but they have an outsized impact on:

- First impressions
- Comfort and usability
- Perceived quality

- Long-term durability
- Overall value

This phase is also one of the safest and most satisfying parts of the Design-Driven DIY approach. The work is forgiving, progress is highly visible, and the payoff is immediate.

*This is not about speed. This is about care, consistency, and pride.*

Rushing now doesn't save time—it creates details you'll notice every day.

## Painting: The Fastest Way to Elevate the Space

Good paint hides small imperfections. Rushed paint highlights them.

Painting is one of the most cost-effective ways to improve your ADU. It protects surfaces, defines style, and makes the entire space feel clean and finished.

### *Interior Painting: Clean, Calm, and Durable*

Interior painting typically happens in two stages: primer, then paint.

Beginner-friendly guidelines:

- Always prime new drywall
- Use quality brushes and rollers (they matter more than paint brand)

- Apply thin, even coats
- Allow full drying time between coats

Color guidance:

***Neutral colors work best for ADUs—especially rentals. They reflect light well, make small spaces feel larger, and appeal to a broader range of people.***

## Exterior Painting: Protection + Curb Appeal

Exterior paint does double duty: it protects the building and sets expectations before anyone steps inside.

DIY-friendly advice:

- Clean surfaces thoroughly before painting
- Use exterior-rated paint only
- Paint during dry, mild weather
- Follow manufacturer guidance for coats and curing

A well-painted exterior instantly increases perceived value—and signals quality inside.

### *Painting Mistakes to Avoid*

☐ Skipping primer

☐ Painting over dust or residue

☐ Thick, rushed coats

☐ Ignoring drying times

☐ Trendy colors that age quickly

Paint is forgiving—if you respect the process.

# Installing Light Fixtures & Ceiling Fans

Lighting changes how a space feels more than almost any other finish.

> Once painting is complete, lighting brings the ADU to life.

## *Installing Light Fixtures*

Most modern fixtures are designed for easy installation once rough electrical work has passed inspection.

Basic steps:

1. Turn off power at the breaker
2. Connect wires by color (black to black, white to white, ground to ground)
3. Secure the fixture to the electrical box
4. Test before final assembly

> *Never rush electrical work. Slow and deliberate is the rule here.*

## *Installing Ceiling Fans*

Ceiling fans improve comfort and reduce energy use—but only if installed correctly.

The electrical box must be fan-rated. Standard boxes are not designed to handle the weight or movement of a fan.

If the box isn't rated, stop and replace it before proceeding.

If wiring looks unfamiliar, confusing, or unsafe—pause.

There's no downside to bringing in a professional for a single fixture if something feels off.

### *Installing Plumbing Fixtures*

Once rough plumbing is inspected, fixture installation becomes a finish task—not a technical one.

Common DIY-friendly installations include:

- Sinks and faucets
- Showerheads
- Bathroom and kitchen fixtures

Keys to success:

- Follow manufacturer instructions exactly
- Tighten fittings carefully (snug, not forced)
- Check for leaks immediately—and again the next day

Most modern fixtures are designed specifically for homeowner installation with basic tools.

## Final Touches: Where the Space Comes Together

Small details don't feel small when they're missing.

This last phase is about cohesion—making sure nothing feels unfinished or accidental.

Your Final Touch List

- Door handles and cabinet hardware
- Mirrors and towel bars
- Window coverings
- Final caulking at joints and transitions
- Paint touch-ups

These details don't take long, but they dramatically affect how complete the space feels.

## The "10-Foot Test"

Stand 10 feet back. If it looks clean, intentional, and consistent—you're done.

If your eye keeps catching the same spot, that's your cue to fix it.

### *Why This Final Phase Matters*

Painting and finish work:

- Create a strong first impression
- Protect surfaces from wear and moisture
- Improve comfort and lighting
- Elevate perceived quality
- Add real property value

This is where patience pays dividends.

## Your Role as the Owner-Builder

The final phase rewards care—not experience.

Your focus now should be:

- Working methodically
- Following instructions closely
- Double-checking details
- Protecting completed work
- Scheduling final inspections when required

When the last fixture is installed and the final coat of paint cures, your ADU stops being a project.

It becomes a place someone can live.

## A Quick Review: Chapter Checklist

Before moving on, confirm:

- ☐ All painting is complete and fully cured
- ☐ Fixtures are installed and tested
- ☐ No leaks or electrical issues remain
- ☐ Hardware and accessories are secure
- ☐ Final caulking and touch-ups are done
- ☐ I know which inspections remain

## Action Steps

- Walk the ADU room-by-room with a punch list
- Install and test one fixture at a time
- Touch up paint after all hardware is installed
- Clean thoroughly before final inspections
- Take photos—you'll want them later

## Scripts & Questions

### *Before Final Electrical Work*

*"Power is off at the breaker, and I'll test everything before closing it up."*

### *Before Final Plumbing Connections*

*"I'll connect this, then check for leaks now—and again tomorrow."*

### *Scheduling Final Inspections*

"All finish work is complete. Can you confirm which final inspections are required before Certificate of Occupancy?"

### *Self-Check Questions*

- "Does this feel finished—or just almost finished?"
- "Would a guest notice this detail?"
- "Is this safe, secure, and clean?"

If the answer isn't a confident yes, pause and fix it now.

## What Comes Next

With painting, fixtures, and final touches complete, you're ready for the final milestone:

Final Inspections & Certificate of Occupancy—the moment your ADU officially becomes a legal, livable home

CHAPTER 13

# SCHEDULING YOUR HYBRID BUILD

In nearly every delayed or over-budget ADU I've reviewed, the root cause wasn't poor workmanship. It was poor sequencing.

Construction projects rarely fail because people aren't working hard. They fail because things happen out of order—materials arrive late, inspections are missed, or the wrong trade shows up before the site is ready.

In a Hybrid Build, scheduling matters even more. You're sharing responsibility with professionals, which means clarity and timing replace constant supervision.

> You don't need a perfect schedule. You do need a clear, realistic one.

A good schedule:

- Keeps momentum going
- Prevents costly downtime
- Reduces stress and confusion
- Helps you plan DIY work around real life
- Protects your budget

Even a simple schedule is far better than no schedule at all.

You're not trying to control everything. You're trying to prevent avoidable delays.

## Why Scheduling Is Different in a Hybrid Build

When there's no full-time GC, clarity replaces control.

In a traditional build, the general contractor manages the entire timeline. In a Hybrid Build, you step into a light version of that role.

That means you're responsible for:

- Knowing when professionals are required
- Scheduling inspections at the right moments
- Understanding when it's safe to begin DIY work
- Avoiding overlaps that create rework

> You don't need construction software or color-coded charts. You need clear phases and realistic expectations.

## The Big Picture: Think in Phases, Not Tasks

Projects move forward in phases—not checklists.

Trying to schedule hundreds of individual tasks quickly becomes overwhelming. Instead, organize your project into five clear phases. Each phase must be completed—and approved—before the next one begins.

### Phase 1: Pre-Construction

- Final plans approved
- Permits issued
- Contractors scheduled

Nothing physical happens yet—but this phase determines how smoothly everything else goes.

### Phase 2: Professional Work (The "Big 3")

Handled entirely by licensed professionals:

- Site preparation
- Foundation
- Framing

Once this phase starts, it moves quickly—but it depends heavily on:

- Inspections
- Weather
- Material availability

### Phase 3: Rough Trades & Inspections

- Rough plumbing
- Rough electrical
- Rough HVAC
- City inspections

Non-negotiable rule: Walls stay open until inspections are approved.

Closing walls early is one of the most expensive mistakes in construction.

### *Phase 4: DIY Interior & Exterior Finishes*

This is where you take the lead:

- Insulation
- Drywall
- Painting
- Flooring
- Cabinets
- Fixtures

This phase takes the longest—but it's also where you save the most money and gain the most control.

### *Phase 5: Final Inspections & Completion*

- Final electrical and plumbing signoffs
- Final building inspection
- Certificate of Occupancy

> This is the finish line. One Phase at a Time

Starting the next phase before the current one is approved almost always creates rework, delays, and frustration.

## A Sample Hybrid ADU Schedule

A good schedule is flexible—but grounded in reality.

Every ADU is different, but this sample timeline gives you a realistic framework:

- **Weeks 1–2:** Site prep and foundation
- **Week 3:** Framing
- **Week 4:** Roof, windows, exterior sealed
- **Week 5:** Rough plumbing, electrical, HVAC
- **Week 6:** Rough inspections
- **Weeks 7–10:** DIY insulation, drywall, painting
- **Weeks 11–13:** Flooring, trim, doors
- **Weeks 14–16:** Kitchen, bathroom, fixtures
- **Week 17:** Final inspections and sign-off

**Reminder**:

DIY usually extends the timeline—but dramatically reduces the budget.

## Coordinating With Contractors (Without Stress)

Contractors work best when expectations are clear, and communication is simple.

### *Before Work Starts*

- Confirm start dates in writing
- Ask how long the work will take
- Clarify inspection requirements

### *During Their Work*

- Stay available for questions
- Avoid changing plans mid-phase
- Schedule inspections immediately

### *After They Finish*

- Walk the work before moving on
- Confirm inspection approval
- Prepare materials for the next phase

Contractor Scheduling Truth: Professionals don't expect perfection. They expect clarity.

## Managing Your DIY Timeline (Be Honest With Yourself)

Most DIY schedules fail because they're built on optimism instead of reality.

DIY work almost always takes longer than expected—especially early on, while you're learning.

***When planning your DIY timeline:***

- Assume evenings and weekends only
- Build in rest days
- Allow time for mistakes and learning
- Order materials early
- Avoid stacking too many tasks at once

A steady pace beats burnout every time.

## Common Scheduling Mistakes to Avoid

- ☐ Starting DIY work before inspections
- ☐ Scheduling trades too tightly
- ☐ Ordering materials late
- ☐ Underestimating drying or curing time
- ☐ Rushing the final phase

Patience saves money—and sanity.

## Your Role as the Owner-Builder Scheduler

Your job isn't to push the schedule—it's to protect it.

**Your core responsibilities are:**

- Tracking progress
- Scheduling inspections
- Communicating clearly with contractors
- Adjusting timelines realistically

A simple calendar, checklist, or spreadsheet is more than enough.

## Why a Good Schedule Protects Your Budget

Delays cost money through:

- Extended tool rentals
- Rework
- Contractor rescheduling fees
- Personal burnout

A realistic schedule keeps momentum going and helps you finish strong.

> Speed vs. Control: Fast projects feel good early. Planned projects finish better.

## Chapter Checklist (Quick Review)

Before moving on, confirm:

- ☐ I understand the five project phases
- ☐ I know when professionals are required
- ☐ I understand when inspections must occur
- ☐ I have a realistic DIY timeline
- ☐ I know how to coordinate with contractors
- ☐ I'm tracking progress in a simple system

## Action Steps (Do These This Week)

- Create a phase-based timeline (not a task list)
- Write down inspection points for each phase

- Confirm contractor availability in advance
- Block realistic DIY time on your calendar
- Add buffer time—you will use it

## Scripts & Questions

### *Confirming Contractor Timing*

"Can you confirm your start date, duration, and which inspection must pass before I move to the next phase?"

### *Scheduling an Inspection*

"This phase is complete and ready for inspection. What's the earliest available date?"

### *Weekly Self-Check Questions*

- "Which phase am I in right now?"
- "Is anything blocking the next phase?"
- "Do I need to order materials this week?"
- "Am I rushing—or progressing steadily?"

## What Comes Next

With a solid schedule in place, the final chapters focus on closing the project successfully final inspections, Certificate of Occupancy, and transitioning your ADU from a construction site into a functioning home.

CHAPTER 14

# BUDGETING & TRACKING COSTS

In most hybrid ADU builds that succeed, the budget isn't smaller—it's clearer.

## Why This Matters

One of the biggest advantages of a hybrid ADU build is cost control. But that advantage only works if you actively track your spending. Most ADU projects don't go over budget because materials are outrageously expensive—they go over budget because costs aren't planned, monitored, or adjusted early.

This chapter shows you how to:

- create a realistic hybrid ADU budget
- track costs without stress or accounting software
- make smart trade-offs before small overruns become big problems

You don't need financial expertise. You need visibility.

### Budgeting Is Not Restriction

A budget doesn't limit your choices.

It gives you the confidence to make them.

## Why Budgeting Is Different in a Hybrid Build

When there's no full-time GC managing costs, awareness replaces guesswork.

In a traditional build, the general contractor controls most of the budget. In a hybrid build, you take on that role, even if only part-time.

A clear budget helps you:

- see where your money is actually going
- decide where to save and where to spend
- avoid surprise expenses
- adjust early instead of reacting late
- finish the project without financial panic

Budgeting isn't about penny-pinching—it's about staying in control.

## Understanding the Two Sides of a Hybrid ADU Budget

Hybrid budgeting works because professional costs are predictable—and DIY costs are flexible.

***Your budget naturally splits into two major categories.***

1. **Professional Costs (Mostly Non-Negotiable)**

These are tasks that must be handled by licensed professionals and usually happen early.

Typical professional costs include:

- design and engineering
- permits and plan check fees
- site preparation
- foundation
- framing
- rough plumbing, electrical, and HVAC

These costs:

- come in larger chunks
- follow a tighter timeline
- leave little room for DIY substitution

2. **DIY Costs (Where You Gain Flexibility)**

DIY costs are spread out over time and allow you to adapt as you go.

Common DIY costs include:

- insulation
- drywall
- paint
- flooring
- cabinets and countertops
- fixtures and finishes

Materials still cost money—but you save significantly on labor.

Why DIY cost feel Easier: You buy them gradually. You control the pace. You choose when to upgra-de—or not.

## A Sample Hybrid ADU Budget (Simplified Example)

Exact numbers vary, but structure stays consistent.

### *Professional Phase*

- Design & engineering: $15,000
- Permits & fees: $8,000
- Site prep & foundation: $35,000
- Framing & exterior shell: $45,000
- Rough trades (plumbing, electrical, HVAC): $25,000

***Subtotal (Professional): $128,000***

### *DIY Phase*

- Insulation & drywall materials: $7,000
- Paint & supplies: $3,000
- Flooring: $8,000
- Cabinets & countertops: $12,000
- Bathroom fixtures & tile: $6,000
- Lighting & electrical fixtures: $4,000Miscellaneous finishes: $5,000

***Subtotal (DIY): $45,000***

***Estimated Hybrid Build Total: $173,000***

Compared to a fully contractor-built ADU, this approach often saves tens of thousands of dollars—without sacrificing quality.

> The Real Win: Hybrid builds don't just save money. They spread costs over time—and reduce financial pressure.

## How to Track Costs

The best budget tool is the one you'll actually update.

You don't need fancy software. A basic spreadsheet works perfectly.

Your Cost-Tracking Sheet Should Include:

- category (e.g., flooring, permits, cabinets)
- budgeted amount
- actual amount spent
- difference (over/under)
- notes

Update weekly.

Small overruns are manageable. Big surprises aren't.

> Track Small Purchases

Fasteners, tools, delivery fees, tax they add up faster than you think.

## When (and How) to Adjust Your Budget

Budgets aren't static—they're decision tools.

Adjust your budget when:

- material prices change
- you upgrade or downgrade finishes
- you hire out a task you planned to DIY
- unexpected site conditions appear

The goal isn't perfection.

The goal is awareness and early response.

### *Common Budgeting Mistakes to Avoid*

☐ forgetting permit or inspection fees

☐ underestimating DIY material costs

☐ ignoring taxes, delivery, and disposal

☐ not tracking small purchases

☐ waiting too long to revise the plan

Every untracked dollar reduces control.

## Your Role as the Owner-Builder (Financially)

Your power comes from knowing your numbers—not guessing them.

### *Your responsibilities:*

- review spending regularly

- compare actual vs. planned costs
- make informed trade-offs
- protect your contingency margin

Good budgeting lets you stay calm—even when surprises happen.

## Why Tracking Costs Pays Off

A well-managed budget:

- reduces stress
- prevents panic decisions
- keeps the project moving
- maximizes return on investment
- helps you finish strong

Hybrid builds reward homeowners who plan carefully and track consistently.

> Control Beats Certainty. You don't need perfect predictions. You need clear visibility.

## A Quick Review: Chapter Checklist

Before moving on, confirm:

☐ I understand the two sides of a hybrid budget
☐ I've listed professional vs. DIY costs clearly
☐ I have a simple cost-tracking system
☐ I know when to adjust the budget

- ☐ I'm tracking small purchases
- ☐ I've built in a financial buffer

## Action Steps

1. Create a master budget spreadsheet.
2. Separate professional and DIY costs clearly.
3. Add a 10–15% contingency line.
4. Enter actual spending weekly.
5. Review budget decisions before upgrading finishes.

## Scripts & Questions

### *Script: Before Making an Upgrade*

"Does this upgrade improve durability or daily use—or just aesthetics?"

### *Script: When Costs Start Rising*

"If this category goes over, where can I save elsewhere without hurting quality?"

### *Questions to Ask Yourself Monthly*

- "Which category is drifting upward?"
- "Do I still have contingency left?"
- "Am I reacting—or deciding calmly?"

## What Comes Next

With your budget tracked and controlled, the final chapters focus on closing the project cleanly—final inspections, Certificate of Occupancy, and transitioning your ADU into use.

CHAPTER 15

# INSPECTIONS, CORRECTIONS & FINAL APPROVAL

In nearly every successful Hybrid ADU build I've reviewed, inspections weren't the obstacle.

They were the confirmation that everything had been done right.

For many homeowners, inspections feel intimidating. Words like fail, delay, or red tag create unnecessary anxiety. In reality, inspections are not designed to stop your project—they exist to make sure your ADU is safe, legal, and ready to be occupied.

If you've followed approved plans and hired licensed professionals where required, inspections are usually routine.

This chapter explains:

- Which inspections to expect
- How to prepare calmly and efficiently
- How to handle corrections without stress
- How to reach your final milestone: the Certificate of Occupancy

Reframe Inspections

Inspectors aren't critics.

They're confirming your work meets the rules that protect you.

## Why Inspections Exist (And Why They're on Your Side)

Inspections don't exist to catch mistakes—they exist to prevent unsafe buildings.

Inspections ensure your ADU:

- Meets current building and safety codes
- Is structurally sound
- Has properly installed plumbing and electrical systems
- Is safe for people to live in

Inspectors compare the work on-site to the approved plans and applicable codes. They are not evaluating your taste, your effort, or your experience level.

Passing inspections means your project meets professional standards—regardless of who installed the finishes.

## The Key Inspections You Can Expect

Nearly all ADU projects follow the same inspection sequence.

Understanding the order helps you stay calm and avoid unnecessary delays.

### *1. Foundation Inspection (Before the Pour)*

This inspection happens before concrete is poured.

The inspector checks:

- Rebar size and placement
- Footing depth and width
- Anchor bolts and hold-downs
- Vapor barrier

Once approved, concrete can be poured.

This is a critical checkpoint—nothing gets buried until it passes.

### 2. Framing Inspection

Occurs after framing is complete and before insulation or drywall.

The inspector reviews:

- Wall and roof framing
- Shear walls and nailing patterns
- Structural connectors
- Beam and header sizes

Passing this confirms the ADU's structural backbone is sound.

### 3. Rough Plumbing, Electrical & HVAC Inspections

These inspections occur before walls are closed.

Inspectors verify:

- Pipe sizes and routing
- Electrical wiring, grounding, and clearances
- HVAC duct placement and safety

Non-negotiable rule:

> Nothing gets covered until these inspections pass.

### *4. Insulation Inspection*

Before drywall installation, the inspector checks:

- Insulation type
- Full coverage without gaps
- Compliance with energy requirements

This inspection is usually quick when insulation is installed correctly.

### *5. Final Inspection*

This is the last—and most anticipated—inspection.

The inspector checks:

- Plumbing fixtures and operation
- Electrical outlets, switches, and lighting
- Smoke and carbon monoxide detectors
- Overall code compliance

Passing this inspection leads directly to final approval.

**Inspection** Order Matters: Skipping or reordering inspections almost always causes delays. Follow the sequence.

## How to Prepare for an Inspection

Preparation—not perfection—is what inspectors expect.

Before the Inspector Arrives

- Have approved plans on-site (printed or digital)
- Confirm work matches the plans
- Provide clear access to inspection areas
- Ensure required utilities are on

A clean, accessible site makes inspections smoother.

First Impressions Count: An organized site signals professionalism—even on DIY-managed projects.

Inspectors notice preparedness.

## What If Corrections Are Required? (Totally Normal)

A correction notice is not a failure—it's part of the process.

Most projects receive at least one correction request. These are usually minor and specific.

Common corrections include:

- Missing labels
- Small nailing adjustments
- Safety clarifications
- Documentation notes

### *How to Handle Corrections Calmly*

1. Read the correction notice carefully
2. Fix only what's listed—no more, no less
3. Document the fix (photos help)
4. Schedule a re-inspection

Most corrections are inexpensive and quick to resolve.

Don't Over-Correct

Fixing things that weren't flagged can create new issues.

Stick to the list.

## The Certificate of Occupancy (Your Finish Line)

The Certificate of Occupancy is the city's way of saying, "You're done—and it's approved."

Once all inspections pass, the city issues a Certificate of Occupancy (CO).

This document:

- Confirms your ADU is legal to occupy
- Allows you to rent or live in the unit
- Marks official project completion

No one can legally occupy the ADU without it.

This is the moment your project becomes a real, usable home.

## Your Role as the Owner-Builder During Inspections

Your job during inspections is coordination—not explanation.

Your responsibilities are to:

- Schedule inspections promptly
- Be present or available
- Provide access to the site
- Communicate respectfully

You don't need to argue or justify decisions.

Show the work. Show the plans. Answer questions simply.

## Common Inspection Mistakes to Avoid

- ☐ Covering work before inspection
- ☐ Deviating from approved plans
- ☐ Missing paperwork or plans
- ☐ Rushing corrections
- ☐ Scheduling inspections too early

Preparation saves time—and frustration.

## Why Inspections Protect Your Investment

Passing inspections ensures:

- Long-term safety
- Full code compliance
- Higher property value

- Fewer future repairs
- Peace of mind

A passed inspection is a stamp of quality, not a hurdle.

Inspections = Insurance

Every approved inspection protects you long after the build is complete.

## Chapter Checklist (Quick Review)

Before moving on, confirm:

- ☐ I understand the inspection sequence
- ☐ I know when each inspection is required
- ☐ I know how to prepare for inspections
- ☐ I understand how to handle corrections
- ☐ I know what the Certificate of Occupancy means
- ☐ I'm scheduling inspections promptly

## Action Steps (Do These Now)

- List all required inspections in order
- Confirm inspection scheduling method with your city
- Keep approved plans accessible on-site
- Photograph work before it's covered
- Treat correction notices as normal—not setbacks

## Scripts & Questions

### *Scheduling an Inspection*

"This phase is complete and ready for inspection. What's the earliest available date?"

### *During an Inspection*

*"Let me know if you need access to anything or the approved plans."*

### *After a Correction Notice*

*"I'll complete the listed corrections and schedule re-inspection as soon as they're done."*

### *Self-Check Questions*

- "Does the work match the approved plans?"
- "Is anything covered that shouldn't be yet?"
- "Have I documented this phase?"

## Crossing the Finish Line

When your final inspection is approved and the Certificate of Occupancy is issued, your ADU is officially complete.

You now have a safe, legal, well-built living space—and the satisfaction of knowing you guided the project with clarity, discipline, and confidence from start to finish.

# CONCLUSION

## YOUR ADU IS FINISHED: WHAT NOW?

ICompleting a Hybrid ADU build is more than finishing a construction project—it's completing a process that most homeowners never attempt.

You planned, coordinated, and navigated a complex system of professionals, inspections, and decisions. You built a fully legal, safe, and livable structure while maintaining control over both the process and the budget. That level of follow-through is rare.

But the real value of this project goes beyond the structure itself.

Through this experience, you developed skills that carry forward: the ability to plan strategically, make informed decisions under real constraints, and manage a large project from start to finish. Those capabilities don't disappear when the construction is complete.

Now the ADU moves into its next phase—serving the purpose you built it for. Whether it becomes a rental unit, a home for family, or a flexible living space, its long-term value will come from thoughtful use and consistent care.

Because you helped build it, you understand this structure better than anyone else. That knowledge is part of its strength.

With proper documentation, routine maintenance, and clear planning for how the space will be used, your ADU becomes more than additional square footage. It becomes a durable asset—one that adds financial, practical, and personal value to your property for years to come.

The Hybrid ADU path may not be the easiest route, but it is one of the most empowering. You stayed engaged, made informed choices, and completed something meaningful.

Your ADU is finished.

Your investment is protected.

And the confidence you gained will last far beyond this build.

Made in the USA
Monee, IL
04 November 2026

67383418R00105